SMALL MINISTRY EXCELLENCE:
Serving as God's Franchise

Dan Mirgon

Dan Mirgon & Associates, Inc.

DAN MIRGON
& ASSOCIATES
Small Ministry Experts

2015

Published by:
Dan Mirgon & Associates, Inc.
PO Box 701343
Salt Lake City, UT 84170
Email: danmirgon@mirgonconsulting.com

Cover Design by: SEM Designs, Salt Lake City, UT

ISBN-13: 978-0692442616
ISBN-10: 0692442618

Printed in the United States of America

Insanity: doing the same thing over and over again and expecting different results.

Albert Einstein

——————— ⊕ ———————

"Do you not know that those who run in a race all run, but only one receives the prize? Run in such a way that you may win."

I Corinthians 9:24

To my wife Sue. Thank you. Without your support and patience this would not have been written

TABLE OF CONTENTS

Introduction   1
LOOKING FOR SOMETHING   3
GOD'S PLAN FOR EXCELLENCE   7
1   Fingerprints   11
3   A Tap on the Shoulder?   15
3   The Inner Bits   19
4   Requirements   23
ARE THERE CRACKS IN THE FOUNDATION?   29
5   Not Your Parents Faith   33
6   Why Bother?   37
7   The Case for Excellence   41
8   "Small" Is Not a Dirty Word!   45
9   Does God Really Need You?   49
A NEW WAY OF DOING "MINISTRY"   55
10 Your Unique Flavor   59
11 Stability, Significance, Legacy   63
12 God's Franchise   71
13 Balancing Faith and Process   75
14 A "Ministry 2.0" Perspective   79
15 The Excellence Components   83
16 How To's   87
17 If We Could Just "STOP!"   93
SERVING AS "GOD'S FRANCHISE"   99
18 The 7 Pillars of Excellence   103
19 Marketing the Franchise   109
20 Funding The Work   113
21 A Board that "Gets It"   117
"A LARGER PODIUM PLEASE"   121
Appendix - A   125
List of References   131

INTRODUCTION

This is not another generic fundraising book that will take up space on your bookshelf. Instead, it is about being the type of ministry that God wants to bless. A Ministry of *Excellence*.

We've written this to help two types of Small Ministry Leaders:

1 – Those who are leading a new start-up ministry we will cover concepts that will help you do it right from the beginning. You will need God's best for your efforts and you don't want to waste time or resources.

2 – Those who are the Executive Director, Board Chair or Development Officer of an existing small ministry and are at a point where something needs to change, this book will help you re-think Ministry in a new way and help you get back on track.

God is most likely doing things through you and your team on a regular basis. You can see Him moving and providing.

But the daily struggle of running the operation seems to always get in the way of "what could be." Sometimes, what was approved at the last board meeting just doesn't fit with the Mission Statement, or some other struggle seems to always hold you back from "getting to the next level."

But what if it's not working the way it used to? Surely there has to be a more productive way to do things.

There is, and that's the reason for this book. It is about giving you a new way to think about Ministry so that the people who are watching are forced to stop and consider this "Christianity" idea in a new way.

Since 1991, we have been helping Evangelical Christian Ministry Leaders build *Stability* into their ministry, turn that Stability into *Significant Impact* for Christ and capture the *Legacy* of what God can do through people who get it right.

The old ways of doing ministry just aren't going to be as effective as they once were. And new for the sake of new isn't the answer either. But there are ways to be more effective and more attractive to a watching world.

We're going to cover topics that some will cheer and others might be uncomfortable with. I promise I'll try to keep the tone upbeat and deal with the painful parts as gently as possible. Unfortunately, over the last 25 years of working with ministries, we've found several areas where small ministries could improve.

The idea is that you should live out your leadership role with the characteristics of a *Humble-Servant-Warrior* who operates God's ministry in a way that allows people to see Christ at work through you.

Wherever you are in your journey and whatever you are struggling with, my hope is that these ideas will inspire you to think about your ministry in a new way - as one of *"God's Franchises."*

Dan Mirgon

LOOKING FOR SOMETHING

Alex loaded the last suitcase into the back of the van. It was another full load and it had already been a long day.

As he helped the young lady take the last empty seat, he couldn't help noticing the pin she was wearing. A gold Cross. "Oh no, not another Bible thumper who wants to save my soul. These religious people are all alike" he thought to himself.

He'd heard it all before, how he needed to "accept Jesus" or that "Christ died for you." "So what? I didn't ask him to do that. Stop trying to push your religion on me."

Alex pulled into the nightmare that was the terminal traffic pattern and headed for the exit.

Through the gate and onto the freeway onramp, he began, "Welcome to Philadelphia. Is everyone in town for the Conference at our hotel?"

Yes - seven passengers all attending the Conference on Biblical Stewardship (whatever that means), he thought.

"Well, it's our pleasure to have you staying with us. May I ask what you all do?"

One at a time, they began.

Tom is the Fundraising Director of an Urban Outreach Ministry, Steve is the Executive Director for a Rescue Mission, Sally runs a Pregnancy Center, Frank is the head of HR for a Retirement Center, Alice raises money for a Camp for Abused Children, Andy works with ex-inmates at an Aftercare program and Oscar is a board volunteer for a Youth Outreach program.

"Well, it's nice to have you with us," he said. Just don't ask me to sign up, he thought.

Driving through freeway traffic, Alex could hear the small talk behind him as the passengers began to get acquainted. Some were excited to see old friends at the conference, others sounded like they had big issues to deal with. A few were quiet – not saying very much. They all seemed hopeful in some way.

As Alex pulled off the freeway and onto the congested city streets, he thought "I'm almost there. One more trip and I can go home for the day."

At the hotel, he quickly opened the back door of the shuttle and began unloading the luggage. As the Bellhop greeted the arriving guests and began loading bags onto carts, Alex looked at each person he had given a ride to. "I wonder if they will find what they are looking for," he thought.

As the passengers thanked him and slipped their "tip" into his hand the young lady with the Cross said something that startled him. "God loves you and wants a personal relationship with you."

Wow! Not the sterile "God Bless" that he had been hearing all day. Not an empty "Bless You" - but "a personal relationship with you." I wonder what that means, he thought.

Maybe she is different. Maybe she knows something that the others don't.

Have you stopped lately to consider how many Alex's are out there – watching every move you make as a Ministry Leader?

I'll bet that if you really knew, it would change how you present your faith.

At the end of the day, the struggle to be effective in ministry and connect with larger audiences is about how much attention you pay to their why – not yours. People do things for their reasons not yours. The only way we can affect real change in someone is to help them want what we want.

Without being too blunt, how attractive is a faith that always points to the sin and doesn't lay out the simple facts of Salvation.

- None of us are perfect
- God can only accept perfect

- Because He loves us and wants a relationship with us, He got off of the bench and came to earth as a man (Jesus)
- He lived a life that was perfect
- He was put to death by us – voluntarily
- He rose from the grave to prove His ability to heal us
- He offers to forgive and forget *all* of our sins
- He promises us perfection in Heaven with Him
- All we have to do is acknowledge that our good will never be good enough
- Put our faith in Jesus and what He did for us - *Forgiveness & Salvation*
- Stop being the idiots we were before – it's not about us anymore - *Transformation*
- Help others hear the "Relationship" story - *Ministry*

That sounds pretty simple right?

Unfortunately, many people might like the "good teacher" or "gentle shepherd" view of Jesus as a person, but most don't like Christians as people.

That's something we must overcome – even among those who claim the name of Christ. As you will read later, a large percentage of them may not be on the same page as you when it comes to what is and what is not Ministry.

GOD'S PLAN FOR EXCELLENCE

"What's He doing?"

"It looks like He's got another one on the drawing board. It seems that He's never finished."

"Who is it this time?"

"I'm not sure yet. I can't see the whole form. Looks like another important one though. He's probably going to spend all day writing this one up too."

"Wow, He sure goes into a lot of detail for each one. I hope they appreciate it."

"Just like the others, He'll give Gabe the final version for safe keeping and spend hours planning for the adjustments – but He knows what He's doing better than anyone."

"He sure seems to care a lot about these people. I hope they understand how much this plan of His will cost Him."

"We'll see. We'll see."

Scripture is very clear about one thing. Someday our Father in Heaven will pull that plan out of some massive filing cabinet and compare what He wrote that day against what actually happened.

I often wonder how my results will look. How about you?

——————— ⊕ ———————

As we think through the concept of Small Ministry Excellence, perhaps we should think about God's plan in a new way. The following outline can help us get started:

What if . . .

1. God's plan is a real blueprint that was written long before we were born

    a. It wouldn't be "Average" it would be "Great"

    b. It is better than you think it is

        i. Excellent

        ii. Professional

        iii. Respected

        iv. Credible

        v. Compelling

    c. That plan has specific things for this ministry and for you to do for Him

        i. You must find out what they are and do them

2. God's plan seeks Excellence

    a. How would He make His plan known to us?

    b. He would be responsible for fulfilling it through us, if we learn what it is

    c. We have to represent Him in a way that draws people to what He is doing

3. God has Called you as a Leader

    a. It is because He wants to do special things in and through you

4. You are in a Leadership Seat

    a. Your character is a real issue. Guard it Carefully

5. You have Followers

    a. They must perceive your confidence and wisdom (whether you feel it or not)

    b. They must see God's hand in the outcomes (they are following God through you)

    c. You have to be able to share God's vision so that they can help you fulfill it

6. That Vision is from God

    a. – He will help you reach it

Now, let's turn our attention to how this outline can come together in your ministry and life.

1 FINGERPRINTS

The NBC Series "CSI" has long been a favorite of a majority of Americans.

With its mix of real science and Hollywood effects the show tries to illustrate what goes into solving crimes. (Does anyone really think it takes 30 seconds to get DNA results?) Its popularity has fostered several spin-offs and has kept us entertained and educated for fifteen seasons.

One of the first investigative tools for fictional and real CSI teams is that of "dusting for prints." The ability to capture the fingerprints of the person or persons involved in the crime quickly narrows the search to those on the list.

But what if we weren't looking for guilt or innocence? What if we were looking for evidence of another kind?

I'm talking about evidence that God is actually involved in a tangible way with what is happening in your ministry. How do we pull our subjective "feelings" or "spiritual discernment" into the tangible world for others to see?

I'm pretty sure the skeptics out there would love it if they could make a personal appointment with God and eliminate some of their questions. Wouldn't you?

Now, we both know God isn't on the other end of a telephone or Skype connection. He's left us all we need to know about life in the Bible, and we'll just have to wait for the Q/A session when we get to Heaven.

But I contend that we can gather the evidence of His presence in some very interesting ways.

First, we should be capturing and documenting the times when no other explanation fits the awesome result that you experienced. You know, when someone drops by the ministry with exactly what you were praying for – before you have made the need known?

Second, allow those times to begin building confidence in you and your staff that God is taking care of you. In your prayer time together, in your staff meetings and at your Board meetings, lay out what happened and watch as others draw the conclusion that your ministry just got visited by God. It's almost as though you can smell His cologne after He's left the room.

Finally, don't get over confident and preachy with this new evidence, but don't hide it either. With a quiet smile and humility, let the person or reader know that "all else being equal, this had to be God's provision or protection or direction. Nothing else explains it adequately."

But looking for and capturing His fingerprints goes even further when we think about all the ways that God is already providing for your needs.

The opportunities to even answer His call came from Him, as did the events that got you into the chair you sit in. No matter how small, I think it is critical that we practice looking at the ministry as His business with His fingerprints on it.

For me, that means that I have a higher call to Excellence and stewardship over what He has called me to do and to manage.

The next time something happens that can only be explained by God's provision or intervention, what will you do with that nugget of Proof?

I really hesitate to suggest that you run through the halls yelling "Look what God did!" They'll think you've slipped a gear.

On the other hand, I think the Humble Leader needs to be prepared to point out, in the appropriate moment, that all explanations aside, God must have just done something.

Start by looking back over the last year or two of ministry. How many times can you identify where this "Only God" explanation fits the scenario?

Write them down and keep them to yourself. Gather as many as you can and read them once a week.

The vision casting that you will be called on to do will require a personal conviction that God really is participating, and in ways that you and your team may not perceive right now.

Then, when a sticky issue comes up, and it will, pull out your list and quietly and humbly begin listing those moments when God stepped in and helped.

If you are comfortable with it, share this idea with a couple of other key Ministry leaders and ask them to do the same.

I'll bet that when you compare notes, you'll hear moments or events that you missed.

What would it be like – in the future – if your Ministry was aware and trained to capture those "God Moments?"

I'm pretty sure the contentment factor within the Ministry would increase and the fear factor would decrease.

Wouldn't that be cool to be part of?

2 A TAP ON THE SHOULDER?

"Something has to be done about . . . . "

"I wish there were a way to . . . . "

"If you make it possible Lord, I'll . . . ."

That's how it starts. You are bugged about something that you clearly feel needs to be done. You already have a plan to accomplish it – if you get the chance. You are being called into ministry.

It may be as innocuous as someone offering you a position in a ministry, something you had never considered, but here is the offer anyway. You are being called into ministry.

In my case and most others, the old saying that God doesn't call the equipped – He equips the called - is true.

That happened to me over 25 years ago. I had built a successful executive benefits business in Southern California. We were on our way to lots of six and seven figure deals when – wham – God changed the plan.

What's your story of how you got involved in a full-time way with God's business? Did you hear a voice, experience traumatic shifts in your career or was it some other method God used?

In all of these settings, God is reaching into our lives and tapping us on the shoulder. He's saying,

"I want you to handle that issue <u>with</u> me."

I'm pretty sure that God has an alarm clock in Heaven set for those who will ultimately end up working in one of His franchises. When that alarm goes off, his blueprint for us is pulled out and the next step in the calling process is set in motion.

Do you remember your call to Ministry?

Some begin their ministry experience reluctantly, not entirely sure that God would be able to use them. Others seek ministry positions only to discover later that they never received the call.

But if you've felt that tap, known the peace of listening to all that God tells you and you are still in your leadership chair, God is clearly not done with you. The question is – how is He planning to use you.

In my case, the income from our financial services company was going to make it possible to write huge checks to God's work. I was going to be the philanthropist. Instead, I ended up a Major Donor and Planned Giving expert for several ministries where we've been able to influence and shepherd many more dollars into the Kingdom than I could have given away in a lifetime.

Others I know entered ministry only because they needed a paycheck and later became convinced that God had directed the steps that got them there. But here they are – leading one of God's franchises.

What is your primary responsibility in this leadership chair you find yourself in?

I believe it involves in large measure the stewarding of God's plan for this ministry and the people involved with it.

Think about that for a minute. The people involved in it. Whom do you think that includes?

Certainly it includes the staff, board and volunteers of your ministry. But we probably should include Donors, vendors, colleagues and the people you serve in that definition as well.

What about their call?

How can we help them identify and clarify their call to ministry? Sometimes we need to ask the "Has this person been called" question sooner when we are hiring staff or recommending a new board member.

But here's a dynamic I wasn't aware of when I started meeting with donors. After hundreds of donor meetings, I've concluded that most ministries determine that if the donor gave once, they'll give again. The relationship is taken for granted.

What if . . . we go ask them why they got involved in the first place?

I've found that most mom and pop donors know subjectively what they like to give to and what turns them off. But when we stop and ask them about how they got connected with us – and then listen, deeply – we begin to hear the real call on their life.

Most of the time, nobody has ever done that with them. When mom or dad express their passions and those passions match up with your mission – that's stewarding your donor into a new awareness of their call to ministry.

It's interesting that the less attention you put on asking for money, the more the relationship is allowed to mature to a point where the focus is off the money and is on the Call for the donor's life.

When the Call and the Vision meet is where the money is. Not before.

3 THE INNER BITS

I'm constantly caught in a conundrum over whether the "Christian" I'm dealing with has a personal relationship with Christ or not. It's a sticky situation that is fraught with risk.

We're not supposed to judge, unless we are willing to be judged in the same way. Most in our culture would also say that we are not to judge at all. Besides, there are a lot of bits and pieces that make up the whole person. Why make such a big deal out of it?

The problem is that not attempting to ascertain the Salvation status of someone is clearly not scriptural or the Bereans wouldn't have been honored with a place in scripture.

If Matthew 7: 13-17 is to be taken literally, there are many who name the name of Christ who are not part of the family of God. That's a sad fact, but a fact none the less. Whether a person has ever acknowledged their utter sinfulness before God, asked that their sins be forgiven and put their faith in Christ for eternal salvation can rightly be doubted if there is no evidence in their life of transformation in Christ.

I would call these people little "c" Christians because they most likely don't have the life of Christ in them yet. They have the trappings of Christianity, but not the relationship. When you get the relationship, you become a big "C" Christian.

On the other hand, neither you nor I are the Holy Spirit and we simply don't know the status of a person's salvation. With that said, we had better be clear about whom we allow on our

Board or whom we hire as part of our staff. You certainly want people who have a passion for your cause, but they need a head for it as well. Most importantly they need to be in the Family.

If we are concerned about the size of their "c" perhaps you should ask deeper questions of yourself and them before moving forward. (Discernment not inquisition)

The Inner Bits of a person who is qualified to participate in the operations of Gods franchise must include Salvation as the core prerequisite ("C"). Otherwise you end up with people whose spiritual discernment is missing and their wisdom is suspect ("c").

The next Bit needs to be an understanding and lifestyle that expresses the characteristics of a *Humble-Servant-Warrior*.

My example is the Centurion in Matthew 8, who came to Jesus asking for his servant to be healed. Do you remember that he went away with only the promise? It's that kind of faith that we all need to be living out. People who understand and live this should be our closest staff, volunteers and board members.

Now, some will say that unless we can find fully functioning and mature "C" Christians we can never move forward on new initiatives or hire staff unless they pass the litmus test. By excluding "c" Christians from important roles in the ministry they think we are being too narrow and extreme.

Those voices are usually the "c" Christians. They believe that Matthew 7 isn't really important. They want a broader tent so that all faiths can participate, so that we can "better understand the people we serve." Their answer will be to become more ecumenical and Faith-Based but it won't be "C."

Stay away from them! (Personally, I like the boldness of saying that we serve Small Christian Ministries instead of Small Faith-Based Ministries. Why pull your punch if you want to have an impact!)

The next Bit is about a personal commitment to whatever God's plan is and whatever their part is in bringing it about.

These folks understand that we can craft the plans and get ready, but at the end of the day, God's will is what we are all after. If He changes the plan, it is because His plans are always better than ours and we need to get over it and move on with what God is doing. Let go of yesterday and live with your eyes on Christ through the windshield – not the rear window.

The final Bit, is an awareness of the fact that God really doesn't need me to do this work. He can get it done with anyone He wants. He has chosen me, not because I'm the most qualified or best on the planet, but because he wants us to do this together – Him and me.

That means I should be doing a lot of listening.

So in the end, you are looking for "C" Christians that have a passion for the work, the professional skills to do the work and who could become the CEO some day – after you are gone.

This might take some adjusting, but you will have fewer problems and higher productivity overall because of it.

You will also be building a community of like-minded *Humble-Servant-Warriors* who can lift each other up when times get tough.

When you think about recruiting new board members or staff or department heads, keep these ideas in mind.

The temptation will be to take the first person that can fog a mirror. Resist this at all cost! It's the beginning of failure and you will spend countless hours trying to undo the effects.

If the person you are recruiting doesn't fit – you'll just have to do without until God provides His selection.

Sometimes you have to look at a lot of rhinestones before you find a diamond.

4 REQUIREMENTS

Humble-Servant-Warrior – The primary focus of those words strung together as they are is to plant in your mind the characteristics that are needed in the Leadership of your ministry, both individually and corporately.

It takes Humility. Knowing that you aren't as good as you look at the moment is an uncomfortable feeling for most of us. In the case of leaders though, looking good at your job can come with the alternative of humility – arrogance and pride.

Genuine humility isn't weakness, and it isn't passivity. It's knowing that you had help getting the result you got and not being so full of yourself that you forget to pass the credit on to the one who deserves it.

That might be your spouse, your staff, your friends, or God. It just means that you aren't the one to take credit for someone else's work.

A Servant's heart is required. Being the one who does the right thing for the right reasons, even when nobody is watching means that you are always mindful of God's presence and are willing to listen close enough to hear even the little requests He has for us.

Imagination is a great asset here as we can so easily forget that He is present wherever we go. My desire to serve His purpose requires I stay close enough to hear what He is asking of me, and then willing to do it – even if it's not comfortable.

Imagine how frequently we need to go back to the throne room for support, instructions and clarification.

Finally, the Warrior characteristic is critical because, like David before Goliath, it isn't our size or reputation that wins battles – it's God's. I've been adopted into His family and He expects me to go into the "Hostile World" and make disciples. That takes courage I may need to borrow from Him.

But that's not all there is to this leadership-ministry thing. It takes plenty of other elements, all pulling together to get this Excellence idea up and running.

It takes Wisdom. Time plus Experience plus Insight can bring perspectives that are desperately needed these days. The idea of "Common Knowledge" isn't so common any more is it?

Wisdom begins with prayer and ends with flexibility. Asking God for direction with a yellow-pad in your hand is generally a good idea here. I recommend writing down everything you are thinking about a topic and then put it away for a while. Go work on something else, and when you return to your pad, see if you still think the same about what you wrote.

Another aspect of wisdom is in getting the insights of other people. Multiple counselors can certainly bring clarity to the message you are hearing. By listening to multiple voices about a single topic, you can hear common threads throughout. These threads can either be for or against the idea, or they may lead you in a direction altogether different than where you were headed.

Unfortunately, too much emphasis can be put into what others have to say. The advisors are not always right, the spreadsheet may have an error in a formula and what your Board or wife think about the idea may not always be from God.

Ask yourself,

"What is the Wise Thing to do in this situation?"

See how it gets answered over time.

It takes Faith. Without Faith, it is impossible to please God. We've all heard that verse used as a justification for not having a plan. We also hear Faith being mocked as "blind-faith" as though our faith in God was leaping into nothingness expecting God to save us from ourselves.

Real Faith, the faith of the Centurion coming to Jesus to heal his servant is always based upon the person of Christ and Word of God.

But in a practical ministry leadership sense, Faith means that we've done all we know to do with the level of Excellence we can pull together. We then present it to God and ask for His blessing, direction and protection. Then we rely on James 4:13-15 for guidance:

Come now, you who say, "Today or tomorrow we will go to such and such a city, and spend a year there and engage in business and make a profit." Yet, you do not know what your life will be like tomorrow. You are just a vapor that appears for a little while and then vanishes away. Instead, you ought to say, "If the Lord wills, we will live and also do this or that."

All of our Strategic Plans certainly need to be drafted, but if God wants to change things up, you had better be willing to adapt. Just because we get comfortable is not a reason to stop listening. It's probably a reason to listen harder.

Also be aware that some people give into the temptation to put God to the test and call it Faith. Like when they don't have the money for something and they write the check anyway or borrow on credit to pay for it. God isn't required to fund plans He didn't initiate. Putting Him on the hook and calling it Faith is just plain foolish.

Finally, the faith of Godly ministry leaders needs to include an awareness and acceptance that God might just do something different than we put into our strategic plan and spreadsheet. I want us to have the faith that says, "He knows what He's doing – and it will be Excellent."

It takes the Right People. Too many ministries suffer from what I call "poverty-think" when it comes to budgets and personnel. Why is that? It's as though we're thirteenth century monks and our poverty makes us more spiritual.

No, ministry done with Excellence requires staff, volunteers and board members that are the best available. Notice I didn't say "that we can afford." Let's start hiring people with the right qualifications and skills for the work that needs to be done.

Have you ever noticed that a professional knows how to work and a minimum wage person usually takes more managing and training? It just makes good business sense. Set your payroll at reasonable levels and set high expectations for the performance of their job. Just like Nike or IBM, you get what you pay for.

As you are recruiting staff, remember the "C" issue as well as the professional requirements. You want Passionate-Professionals who get the big picture of working in God's Franchise.

It takes Prayer.

Regularly going before Dad is where all of our planning and management effort must begin and end. You need to seek His will, His provision, His leading, His glory, His protection and a few thousand other things.

As one of the Ministry Leaders, your *Humble-Servant* role requires that you have a functional and rich prayer life. God wants to be part of every decision that you make.

I recommend that you also seek out several private prayer partners who are willing to share the load before God with you. You will need people you trust to keep confidences and they will need to be kept informed about whatever the prayer list includes.

They will most likely include some inside the ministry, but don't limit yourself to insiders. You need external partners as well. Have no other agenda with these people except for their participation in the prayer process.

You need to remember that this ministry is His Franchise and you are responsible for His reputation. You need His help to pull that off so that others see Him and want to join in what He is doing.

That's where it gets exciting!

ARE THERE CRACKS IN THE FOUNDATION?

Something bad happened a while back and none of us got the memo.

If you were a ministry leader in 2007 you probably joined your peers and took a collective deep breath as the candidates for the Presidency of the United States became clearer. Whichever side of the political fence you are on, neither choice presented much hope for real change in a direction that most of the country wanted.

About that time most ministries, both big and small, began rethinking how they did business.

Many went and hid in the back of the cave, waiting for the upcoming political storms to settle down. Others trimmed expenses and got leaner, hoping that the forecasts weren't going to come true. Many others simply didn't think it was going to be as bad as it got and are not here anymore.

Regardless of which choice you made, you've had to deal with a rapidly declining "admiration" for Biblical Christianity at all levels since then. In effect, the Christian World view that America was founded upon has been put on suicide watch with no end in sight.

The fuse was lit. It's as though that "admiration" has degraded to "tolerance" and is on its way to "elimination" unless God intervenes.

It seems as though the entire world is now in great fear of almost everything – distracting your audience from the great work God is doing though you. The cultural slide has shaken most small ministries down to their roots and eroded the support and goodwill they had before.

What about you? Is the partnership with Christ on which your ministry's confidence rests shaken? I hope not.

Many small ministries have been able to pull all the components together and accomplish great things for the Kingdom. Whether there was adequate funding or not, ministry is still getting done and people are being brought to a place where they can hear and accept the offer of a new life in Christ.

If you feed the hungry, it is so that they can hear about life-transformation in Christ. If you heal the sick and wounded, or teach the unlearned, or counsel the confused – the end purpose should be the same.

Whatever method your ministry uses - the end goal hasn't changed.

Inviting people to know Christ through repentance and faith is "Ministry" of the highest order. Everything else is, or should be, the path to that moment in time.

Matthew 29:19-20 is the Scripture that gives us our "Marching Orders."

Jesus is about to leave for Heaven, not to return physically until we meet him in the clouds. As he lays out the plan for the Disciples and his followers, He gave only one option on how to follow His orders.

He said,

> *"Go therefore and make disciples of all the nations, baptizing them in the name of the Father and the Son and the Holy Spirit, teaching them to observe all that I have commanded you; and lo, I am with you always, even to the end of the age."*

He left the interpretation of those orders to us to some degree. As a result, over two-millennium later, we have thousands of individual "Para-Church ministries" who all should be working on fulfilling the same marching orders, yet in your own way.

So, how are you doing? Is the "Foundation" of your Operation cracking under the workload? Do people perceive you as a partner with the God of the universe?

If your ministry has it "all together" and nothing is wrong – praise God, and look out because something will change. It always does.

But what if your audience can't sense that God is working through you anymore? This culture is already trying to quiet the voice of effective Christians. Are you going to be one of those ministries that get less and less attention?

What would happen if your ministry was so effective and run with such Excellence that they had to pay closer attention?

That is what you are up against. But you will need an effective plan of action to bring people to a point where they have to reconsider God's present day involvement in this world's activity. To do that, we need to bring a new professionalism to our ministry and break the stereotypes that have such a stranglehold on people's perceptions.

We need a new way to think about ministry.

Enter the "Franchise" idea.

In a world that resists and ridicules Christianity, you need to remember that when God is involved though the Ministry, you are serving as an outpost of Heaven.

This "Franchise of God's Business" concept might sound like nothing more than a catchy way to sell books, but if you think it through – you are running His business. His operation to serve the people you serve.

Any Franchise deserves some serious thought about how it represents Headquarters to a world that thinks He's irrelevant.

That's the where thinking about your ministry as aFranchise can help. Your Ministry is not your own – it's His. It requires an approach that says, "As a steward of His business, how can I represent His interest best?"

I'm pretty sure that God wants to bless His Ministries when they are seeking to please and glorify Him.

5 NOT YOUR PARENTS FAITH

I was born in the middle of the 1950's (there, I said it. I'm an old guy). Those were the days of Ozie and Harriet, Howdy Doody, Bonanza, the Lone Ranger and Sky King.

Life was pretty much in black and white (including your TV set). You were either a Christian of some version, or a heathen. The American culture still had a large portion of "Old World Christianity" ingrained in it and people knew a lot about the Bible and Christian history whether they subscribed to it or not.

Fast forward to the sixties where the Cold War, Civil Rights, Rock and Roll, Viet Nam were all we heard about from the media. These headlines gave society permission to "progress" into a "better future" that was not well defined.

Push the button again and the seventies, eighties and nineties fly by in a drug-induced blur of self-absorbed children crying for "their rights" and wanting anything but the limitations of a Sanctified life. The Bible couldn't be true and surely there was more to life that we could experience without God. (Sounds like Genesis 3 all over again)

The turn of the twenty-first century gave us *Relativism* on steroids and normalized the "anything goes" selfishness to a point where now, to have any objective standard of truth makes you the enemy. Historical truth is reduced to individualized truth.

Oh yeah – don't forget to be tolerant of the beliefs of others. You might offend someone.   It seems in an attempt to be more tolerant – the culture is tolerating everything except the Bible and Bible believing Christians.   Has Christianity lost its influence in American culture?

It has, according to George Barna.   His book, *The Seven Faith Tribes*, states, *"More than four out of every five adults in America consider themselves to be Christian."*

That means that eighty percent of this country claims to be Christians.   A quick look at the news from any media outlet would lead us to wonder where these "Christians" are hiding. They certainly aren't influencing the culture for Christ.

Barna goes on in the book to indicate that of the eighty percent of Americans that claim to be Christians, *"Most of the country's self-described Christians . . . fit within the Casual Christian Tribe."*

He describes the Casual Christian as,

"Casuals are tethered to a set of core values that dictate their behavior and attitudes, yet they remain very open to a wide array of moral perspectives and lifestyles.

They do not consider this to be caving into social pressure as much as satisfying their desire to get along with others and to experiment with new options.

They claim to support "traditional family values," but are equally as prone to adopting nontraditional viewpoints in order to stay connected to other people and to remain at peace with the world."

In other words, two-thirds of the people that we perceive as "Christians" are open to other ideas about morality, faith and ministry – beyond what Christ asked us to focus on.

That should scare you to death! It should also wake us up to a very real fact:

The American Culture thinks God is dead (or irrelevant) and you are an Idiot for following Him!

So here is my question.

What are we doing to show your fellow believers and the unsaved world that God is still participating in the world today?

I'm not talking about what you say as much as your need to point to His work and give Him the credit.

But you will also need to give Him the credit in ways that actually make sense to the audience you are speaking to.

Putting on some huge media event to prove your point or trying to persuade people that your view of God is accurate and theirs is not just isn't going to cut it anymore.

It's still Gods job to persuade people – but it is your job to get them into the conversation.

But there is another problem. Our language isn't their language. When you or I speak Christianeese to a person that hasn't signed up for our faith, we alienate them.

We need to speak in ways (minus the f-bombs) that connect with the people we are trying to influence. We must present the reality of Christ and the Transformational result of a relationship with Him in a way that makes academic, emotional and personal sense.

Personal stories help a lot here. *"I don't know about you, but I believe that God did something that simply can't be explained any other way."*

We are half way through the second decade of the twenty-first century. Shouldn't we rethink how we are displaying God and His present day activity so that the world has to reconsider their conclusions?

What if that's what He wants us to do?

So, of your donors, volunteers, staff and prayer partners, how many do you think could be considered "Casual" by Barna's analysis? How do you know?

Hopefully, it's not as many as you think. But what if it is more than we believe? Is the way you run the Ministry doing anything to draw people to new perspectives about God and His involvement?

6 WHY BOTHER?

Very often we hear a ministry leader say the following:

"We're doing okay. We don't need to do anything differently."

In other words, if it doesn't seem to be broken at the moment, why run the risk of breaking it?

Congratulations! You must be doing fine and you don't feel the need to spend time and money rehashing what's already been done. If you really are at that point, we are glad to hear it. I hope things really are "okay."

You see, many ministries have said, "we're fine" only to find out that there were glaring issues staring them in the face that needed to be addressed.

Whether the underlying issues caused by lack of awareness, personal ego, or some other malady, very often, Leaders mistakenly believe that "everything is fine."

But when you interview the staff or the Board, something is out of alignment. People are walking on egg shells about some topic that needs to be addressed.

The uncomfortable – elephant in the room is Change.

Change is a scary thing and some people just can't handle it. Change, or the idea that something isn't already perfect, can lead us to do all types of strange things.

We like things as they are, pretty much. This idea that we can and should do better is forcing us to face certain realities about ourselves that, for now, haven't been big enough to require attention.

But what if God's blue print for you calls for more?

In his bestselling book, *The Shack*, author Paul Young tells the story of change from a perspective that makes it clear that most people are more afraid of what the change might look like than they are the outcome of the change. This "fear of change" is sometimes bigger than the courage it takes to face it.

Many of us are more comfortable with what we know – warts and all – than we are with what the unknown would mean. As a result, ministry leaders resist evaluating their Ministry for fear that the changes that might be required will be things they can't control or will be "uncomfortable" to those who work there.

There is no perfect solution to that dilemma, but I'm going to make the case for being open to change through the Evaluation process anyway.

In the same way that you check the air in your tires and the oil in your engine, healthy ministries actually take a look under the hood once in a while. They have plans and processes set up to review their ministry regularly.

The real question for those that don't is what might be gained by taking a long deep look into all the aspects of how the ministry is Lead, Managed and Funded – just to make sure nothing is waiting there that needs to be fixed.

So, what happens if you find something that you don't like?

Fix it before it gets big and threatens your stability. That's what a *Humble-Servant-Warrior* would do.

How often you evaluate things is up to you, but part of effective strategic planning is the process of regular evaluation as well. Evaluation should be done at least annually, but that's not a hard and fast rule. Just don't get five or ten years down the road before you get to it.

There is one more pretty important reason to ask the "Why Bother" question.

Imagine a time at the Reward Ceremony in Heaven when your ministry's name is called. Everyone who has given financially, served, volunteered and prayed for this ministry will get a reward.

Now picture what that reward might look like. I'm imagining a cup with handles on its sides set into a base with my name engraved on the plaque.

But what might God put inside the cup? Have you ever considered that the "Excellence" question has more to do with what is put in the cup than whether you get a trophy or not? Think about that for a minute. If lower performing, average ministries get "stuff" put in their cup - what would Excellent ministries get?

See, I think God is not only concerned with whether we run the race to win (I Corinthians 9) but with how it was done. Did we do it with style? His style? Did His Excellence shine brightly for the entire world (your audience) to see?

The reason to review your ministry on a regular basis is the same reason professional strategic plans include evaluation in the first place. If something is changing – you need to know it sooner than later.

If it's an opportunity, jump on it! If it's a problem, jump on it!

Here is where the *Warrior* characteristic comes in. You need the courage and the faith of the Centurion in Matthew 8.

The courage to leave your assigned post to take care of something critical in your life (Ministry). He might have had the day off, but more than likely, he ran the risk of being accused of consorting with the enemy of Rome (the Jews).

But he also had the faith that knew that whatever God wanted was worth the risk. The *Humble-Servant-Warrior* kicked in and he stepped out of what was "comfortable" and "asked for the impossible."

Are you willing to do the same? Remember, Jesus honored him by not only including his story in the Bible, but He healed the servant and said that He (Jesus) had not seen such faith in all of Israel.

How comforting is this story when you are considering taking on serious challenges in the Ministry? I'll bet the Centurion went away believing that God's word was reliable and this probably changed his life forever.

7 THE CASE FOR EXCELLENCE

Have you ever shot an arrow at a target? Remember that hay bale with the target pinned to it almost two city blocks away – and you are supposed to hit it with this piece of wood in your hand?

I had my first experience with a real bow and arrow as an eleven year old at Boy Scout camp. Man was that an experience!

Not only was the bow heavy and the string hard to pull, but wow – did that hurt when I let go. The string scraped across my arm and to this day, I can't remember whether I hit the target or not.

I've been shooting at targets metaphorically all my life. So have you.

As I've gotten older though, I've figured out that no matter what you go through to get the arrow down range – the goal is to hit the target in the center for a bull's-eye. Hitting the bull's-eye, the "Mark", is what the effort is all about.

So I had this thought one day that changed how I did life.

If I shoot at Average and miss, what do I hit?

That one got to me.

Do you remember elementary school where your first social skill was fitting in?

For most of us, being "normal" gave us a sense of comfort and belonging. "Normal" was "Average" and you sure didn't want to be Below Normal. I think for most of us, those early days pushed us into accepting "Average" as the goal and only an exceptional few were permitted to work towards "Above Average." No, average was the goal for most people in the second grade.

Some of us though, seek after Excellence so that we can rise above "average" and improve our options in life. Not a bad thing to teach our children. "You get out of life what you put into it", and other concepts drive most of the entrepreneurial spirit in America and around the world.

But how does that impact running a Christian Ministry as an adult?

Well, it seems pretty intuitive but when you miss *Average*, you hit *Below-Average*. It takes the same amount of effort to aim at *Average* as it would to raise your sights and aim for *Above Average* – but for some reason, *Average* becomes the acceptable target.

> *So in God's economy, what happens if we re- think Average, and aim for Excellence? (The Mark)*

This perspective takes the spotlight off of our self-defined view of Excellence, and places it on His Divinely inspired definition of Excellence.

Please don't hear me say that trying to get ahead in your personal life is wrong. That's not the idea here. Rather, the idea I'm presenting looks at Ministry specifically and forces you to put your personal perspective down and take up God's perspective on what He wants to do in and through this ministry you are running.

I believe that God has a Blueprint for each of us that includes His Best Plan for you. How closely we follow that plan determines the reward at the Ceremony in Heaven.

But if God has a specific plan with your name on it, He probably also has a plan for His Franchise that you are serving in.

The question is, what are we doing to discover and live out those plans? What could happen if we align ourselves with God's ultimate plan for this ministry?

I believe that God wants us to turn our attention to fulfilling His plan rather than touting our ability to help Him accomplish the work. When we do that, He blesses His work because we aligned ourselves with His Plan. We let Him lead. We follow.

Isn't it ironic that God's word for missing the "Mark" is Sin? Maybe He knows something about our struggles with achievement and worth.

What would it look like if you . . .

- Stopped and fixed the areas of your Operational Plan that had missing or broken parts?

- Allowed God to reveal your next move and focused on doing the "Current Plan" better than ever?

- Were realistic about the number of people you can serve with Excellence and trust God to take care of the ones you can't – right now.

Now if you do that, what can you expect?

First, not everyone on your team will be a fan of the new plan. Remember, change only happens when enough people catch a compelling vision and work toward its fulfillment.

So, you might just have to start slowly. Begin speaking about doing better without making it a "Quality Improvement" program. All that programs ever do is make people think that you are going through a "Phase" and you'll get over it.

Rather, you may have to begin modeling that Excellence. Then, start capturing what God is doing and point people to the evidence. Ultimately, they will start to understand.

The path to Excellence begins with you and ends in Heaven. It will not be simple, but it will be worth it.

You will know you are on that path when new donors show up without any way of identifying their source. When issues that were roadblocks yesterday, become opportunities today.

When people start asking, "Is there a better way to do this" without your prompting.

8 "SMALL" IS NOT A DIRTY WORD!

Growth! It seems to be all the rage today. In fact, a Google search for "Business Growth" will bring up a mere 12,000,000 listings. "Ministry Growth" gets 23,500 listings on 46 pages.

From all that information, you would think that Growth was a pretty big deal. So let's all get on the band wagon and Grow – Okay?

Wait, what? Is God asking you to grow? What kind of question is that? Everybody knows that growth brings in more money and will allow you to serve more people. Who wouldn't want you to grow?

Well, God might not want you to grow.

In today's business environment, getting to the next sale and keeping your brand top-of-mind is how businesses survive. Every day, secular businesses need to push the envelope and keep the peddle-to-the-metal just to keep up with the "Strategic Growth Plan."

What would it look like if God actually wanted your ministry to stay small? Have you ever considered that as an option? Remember, you are not a secular business.

I believe that most small ministries would do better if they spent whatever time and energy you have – to just do great work. Get everything ready for the future – but do it by being the best you can possibly be with that you currently have.

When it's time to grow, God will begin bringing new opportunities and new resources to the table and will show you pretty clearly that He thinks you are ready.

Until then, I believe we honor Him better when we are content with what we have and use it to provide Excellent programs, hire quality staff, have adequate systems and collectively spend time thanking Him for providing as much as He has.

This is where the Organizational Character comes in. If you are operating one of God's Franchises, the standards should be pretty high for customer service (Donors, Guests, and Volunteers) financial accountability, Godly leadership and Christ-like unity.

These things point to God as the author and originator of His ministry, and to our ability to be Humble in our service to His plan.

So, what are the advantages and disadvantages of being small versus growing?

For one thing, small ministries can focus on doing what they do really well. They (you) can become known as the place to go when you need it done right.

Additionally, people want to support exciting, impactful and meaningful ministries. Small – the size you are now – just may be where you are supposed to be.

Without being pulled in too many directions, you can focus on doing exactly what is needed for each client, guest, patient or member. They might actually feel like you were taking personal time with them so that you could best meet their needs.

Do you have to stay there? No. But we've both seen companies and ministries outstrip their ability to do quality work because they grew before they were ready.

Here is the meat of this idea. If God wants you to grow, He will most likely allow you the time to get really good at what you do. He will then send you far too many people to serve because you followed His lead as to when to grow. Finally, if He is pushing you to grow – don't fight it. He will fund it.

What about the disadvantages of being a small ministry.

Well, you don't have to stretch your staff too thin, and you miss out on having to look for space, and you won't have to decide who to hire and how to pay for all of this new stuff. Bummer!

Being content with what God sends your way and allowing Him to push the growth button allows you the freedom to focus on Excellence.

Do it right – repeat – wait – repeat.

9 DOES GOD REALLY NEED YOU?

The last time I looked, God isn't waiting for me to do something for Him in order for His plan to get accomplished. I know - that's disappointing for some of us, but it's the truth.

In the book titled *TrueFaced*, the authors tell a tale of a journey in search of our dreams. Some are from God, and some are from us – but they drive us to accomplish things none the less.

The interesting point of the book is that in our struggle to eliminate sin, become more holy, be better Christians and more – we can simply forget the one attribute that God wants from us. Faith.

Now, I know that we don't get out of bed in the morning without exercising faith, but what I'm talking about is that vision fulfilling, ministry starting, God honoring thing we call faith.

Unfortunately, I can sometimes put my faith into things that don't matter. In the context of this chapter though, let's think about our faith in what we do for God through ministry.

Does it really matter if I'm doing it or if someone else is doing it?

The question of whether God need us could put some people off. Since the majority of readers of this book will be working in ministry, let's think through that question this way.

Is God able to accomplish His purposes without you or this ministry? Obviously, the answer is yes! God is able to do what He needs to do in ways that we may not understand or see.

But He allows us to play along. He offers us a spot on the Podium in Heaven when the awards are handed out for this ministry's impact for Christ.

For me, this means that whether I fully understand it or not, God is working to accomplish His plan and is allowing me to participate. I get to be His hands and feet while We (He and I) accomplish whatever is on the agenda today.

If I'm serving in this ministry, trying my hardest to please Him with my service – and it turns out that He's got another plan – I'd be wasting His time and my effort if I don't pay attention.

I know this because I've seen it happen in my own life and in some of the ministries we've served.

When I as travelling as a major donor representative for a large international missions organization, I remember a donor visit one evening.

An elderly couple in their 90's had served in the jungles of the Amazon for over 60 years and were telling story after story of life with "their people" in South America. I remember thinking that I was there to ask for a financial investment in one of the projects that needed support – but I was really there to pray with them about whether God wanted them to return "home" and die where they had spent their life.

Now I don't usually pray with major donors about where they will ultimately die, but in this case, my agenda became completely unimportant and was replaced with God's agenda of encouraging this elderly couple. Right then, that evening, they needed to hear that God knew where they were supposed to be and we all agreed that if they couldn't go "home," then God would provide someone else to continue their work.

Did God need me for that? Not necessarily. He could have dealt with it in any number of other ways. But I was there – and available. He allowed me (gave me the faith) to see that my agenda wasn't why I was there that evening – but His.

But what happens in ministry when we forget faith or worse yet, try to live only from faith?

This is where Luke 14: 28-30 comes in.

> *"For which one of you, when he wants to build a tower, does not first sit down and calculate the cost, to see if he has enough to complete it? Otherwise, when he has laid a foundation, and is not able to finish, all who observe it begin to ridicule him, saying 'This man began to build and was not able to finish.'"*

Whose reputation is at stake here? Yours – certainly, but more importantly, **God's reputation is at stake when we don't present His ministry as though He is involved**.

We'll spend some time on this concept in a later chapter – but your ministry should be thought of as "Gods' Franchise" in your local community. How is His reputation perceived by the viewing world based on how you are running it? It could be good or could be bad – right?

So it seems there are two extremes we need to be aware of and guard against.

First is the extreme of "Faith Only." You know these people. They shun strategic planning and fundraising by citing historical characters like George Mueller as evidence that "God will provide" as their business plan. (If you've read any of his presentations you know that he always told people how much he needed, but always ended with "But God will provide")

The problems with this simplistic approach are many.

First, without a plan, how will you know if God is changing direction? Have you ever taken a road trip with your entire family? The question of where you want to go that day can quickly become a nightmare until someone (preferably the driver) decides that "East" is better than "South."

Likewise, you'll never fulfill your mission because you don't have a roadmap. How will you gather financial support for a vision that can only be fulfilled if everyone has your level of faith? That simply will never happen.

You need a compelling plan to draw your audience to. You need a credible and current Strategic Plan that everyone believes is part of God's blueprint for your ministry.

Second, you have no credibility with donors who could make significant gifts to the ministry. You'll be a beggar the rest of your days. How many times have you received an appeal from a ministry that is about to go out of business – unless you send them $14.95? Do you really think that your small gift will solve anything?

To reach new audiences and cultivate larger gifts from existing ones, you need a professionally crafted Marketing and Fundraising plan that uses every tool in the toolbox to reach more people this year than you did last year. They need to hear about how God is reaching more people through you and this ministry because of their partnership with Him.

Finally, and most the concerning, the unsaved world will continue to think you are an Idiot! Remember – Alex and his peers didn't sign up for your faith – and you might just want to evaluate whether your version is attractive to them or not.

But without a concerted effort to change the dialogue, the secular culture, led by the enemy of your soul will continue to paint every Christian as a buffoon.

The other extreme is made up of the "Process Only" group. Here we have an overdependence on yesterday's "Procedures." Spreadsheets and budgets make all the decisions.

They cite DL Moody and his direct mail campaigns as evidence that process is king. (By the way, Moody prayed over each appeal and relied on God's provision – but hey, let's not get off track)

Oh, this group will develop a strategic plan and then put it on the shelf in the Executive Directors office as a trophy to times long ago when "God gave us this direction." Or worse, they can't see past the spreadsheet to recognize new opportunities when God presents them.

Here's the problem. Without evaluation and review, how do you know whether God is changing the "plan" or not? What if He wants to bless you, but you won't let Him because it's not "in the budget" or "the board will never agree to this."

For any ministry to be attractive to major and annual donors, there are three characteristics that must be in place.

1. An Important Cause

2. Credible Leadership

3. Concern for Your Future

All three of these will be expanded in a later chapter, but for now, if you don't present a credible case for support, illustrate your ability to hit the goal, and can't tell stories of how God is using your ministry to reach people for Christ – then you should go get a job outside of ministry. Period.

One other scripture needs to be reviewed in light of these issues: 1 Corinthians 9:24 tells us,

> *"Do you not know that those who run in a race all run, but only one receives the prize? Run in such a way that you may win."*

It's pretty clear that between these two passages, we are to have a plan to win. We are required to seek Excellence so that God's reputation can be on display. The Alex's of the world need to see that there is something different in you. Something they don't have – and need to find out about.

That's what Christ was talking about on the Mountain Top.

That's Ministry!

A NEW WAY OF DOING "MINISTRY"

The legendary Basketball Coach, John Wooden once said,

"If you don't have time to do it right, when will you have time to do it over?"

What if you had the opportunity to start over? What would you do differently?

I think Madison Avenue marketing has infected the storytelling of Secular Charities and Christian Ministries and has given them a bad image these days.

In the world of secular fundraising, playing to images of emaciated puppies and homeless veterans blend into one loud voice of "we need your money or we'll go out of business." The impact the money has on individual lives is always an afterthought in the 30 second commercial.

Christian ministries aren't immune from media manipulation either. Many seem to be always offering some type of "blessing" as the reward for helping them stay afloat, or some other appeal to be rescued from their bad planning and lack of Stewardship. Either that, or they're making you feel bad that you haven't "rescued the hurting soul" yet.

As of this writing, it is 2015. Nobody with a clue about economics believes that we are in a "Stable Economy" and the impact on fundraising hasn't been the same since 2007.

So, as funding gets harder to find, does it make sense to do the same things – or worse yet – try harder with old tactics?

Here's my thought. What if the issue is that we need to operate differently? What if we need to be so different than secular organizations that people have to take you seriously? I'll bet you would do that if you could.

To make this happen, let's drill down on the Non-Profit vs. For-Profit idea. Here's what I mean.

What is the one singular difference between a Non-Profit Organization (NPO) and a For-Profit, say Apple or IBM?

Both the NPO and the For Profit have to incorporate to be taken seriously. They both have to file returns with the IRS. They both have to keep accurate books and records. They both have to market their services or products. They both need quality professionals at the helm, leading the charge for market share and profitability.

Oh, wait! I used the "P" word. (Not sorry – you'll see why in a minute)

I'm afraid that for a majority of people, the acronym NPO translates into just another organization that is after my money.

But what if you and I were to redefine that right now, okay? What if tomorrow morning when you come to work, NPO meant something different; something fresh?

How do you feel about:

New - *Professional* - *Organization*

Would that shake things up a bit at your next Board Meeting?

But we can't Dan – we don't pay taxes. Yep – you're right.

You don't pay taxes and as a result, the IRS gives your donors a tax deduction when they make a gift.

News Flash!   That's the only difference between you and a for-profit company. In exchange for not paying taxes, you are supposed to use those "profits" (the money you don't pay in taxes) to help people get what the government can't provide and won't provide.

Ladies and Gentlemen – you need to run your ministries as though you are competing against Wal-Mart, Time Warner Cable, and Kroger because, you are! Who doesn't think that the normal donor to your ministry might have to go without something if they make a larger investment in your latest project?

Let's get real here. You are competing against everything that makes up a donors monthly budget. Why on earth should a person go without that extra latte so that you can do that thing you do for someone who needs it?

The only answer that makes sense is that people will give when they feel that their investment is connecting with what God is doing through you.

Now for the fun part! Because you don't have to pay taxes, you are supposed to be able to reach more people per dollar than a for-profit might, and . . . because you are connected with God – your donors want to participate. The donors want to be part of God at work!

So go to work tomorrow with a Cheshire grin on your face and begin looking for ways to re-engineer the ministry to align with this vision. I'll bet you get a lot of funny looks – but then you have a new story to tell.

10   YOUR UNIQUE FLAVOR

Have you ever heard people make statements about God doing partial work or not completing what He started? Statements like "partial healing" or "God started creation with the Big Bang" and other statements make me wonder about that person's view of God.

I'm sure you remember the scene at Christ's crucifixion don't you? When the sun went dark, the earth shook, and the temple curtain was torn from the top to the bottom. Jesus is breathing his last breath, He cries out, *"IT IS FINISHED!"*

Aren't you glad He didn't say, "It will be finished when . . . "or "Almost done dad!"

Now, I come from the school of theology that says that in the absence of contradictory passages, we are to take what is written in the Bible literally. God told Moses to part the Red Sea and it parted. How God did that is not all that important – unless I'm trying to minimize his sovereign Deity. (A small view of God requires a strong wind and a submerged land bridge)

For me, that means God must be big enough to have created both the universe and us in the literal six days Genesis outlines. And if He is big enough to do that – He must be capable of pretty much anything He wants to get done, including helping us understand how to play along without messing up His plan.

So when it comes to running a small Christian ministry, why do so many feel that without our help, God can't do something? ("He can't return until all the languages are translated" or "no one will take care of them if we don't")

Parting oceans, making donkeys speak, healing people, rising from the dead, changing Dan Mirgon from who he was – doesn't really seem all that impossible when you look at God from that perspective.

How about we dare to speak heresy and think about our ministries in new ways?

I'm sure you remember the old story of the young married couple and the roast. The husband comes home from work to see his lovely bride preparing dinner. She is seasoning the meat (a rather expensive roast) and before she puts it in the oven, she takes a large butcher knife and cuts one end off of the roast and throws it away.

Curious, the husband asks why she did that. "I don't know, that's what my mom always did."

At the next family holiday, the young husband sees Mother-In-Law do the same thing to her roast. Again he asks, and is told, "Oh, that's how my mother always prepared the roast."

Wanting to get to the bottom of "the case of the wasted meat" he goes into the living room where "Grandma" is sitting. Summoning up his courage, he asks, "Ohm a, I've watched my wife and her mother preparing roasts, and I'm curious. They both cut the end off of the roast before cooking it. May I ask if you know why they do that?" Grandma shrugs and says, "That's how I always did it too. My roasting pan was always too small so I had to make it fit."

The point is that just because we have done it a particular way, or "this is how non-profits do it" – doesn't mean you need to do it that way too. In fact, (here's the heresy);

What if your ministry is supposed to be unique, a one of a kind, not a knock-off of some other ministry?

Oh sure, there will be similarities of how you and another ministry do their work, serve your people and so forth. But what makes us think that we have to use the "Association's model" for everything? What if that's only a baseline from which we branch out and allow God to lead us in His direction?

It's like making gravy from scratch. You and I might use similar ingredients and cooking techniques, but my gravy will taste different than yours. If we are all using the same packaged mix to make the same gravy – there is absolutely no reason for a donor or volunteer to join in your efforts because there will be nothing unique about your "flavor."

Under that scenario all ministries are the same. Why should they care about you? But maybe even more damaging is the idea that we might be missing out on what God wants to do – if we limit ourselves to "what we know and understand."

11   STABILITY, SIGNIFICANCE, LEGACY

To make sure that we don't end up tasting like everyone else's gravy to our audience, let's begin to unpack the three characteristics that can set your ministry apart from the crowd.

STABILITY

You will need to start by focusing on the STABILITY of your Ministry. In this phase, you fix any cracks in your "operational foundation" and settle into a rhythm of operating every aspect of the ministry with Excellence and quality.

"What if . . . . " I love those types of questions because they begin with possibility as the premise.

What if your ministry was stable in all the areas it needs to be?

- There was enough money to meet the needs (not the wants)

- There were qualified professional staff people doing the work that you didn't have to babysit all day

- There were a group of Board Members who saw their job as both Trustees and Resource Gatherers

- Your Donors were rabid evangelists for your ministry to their friends

- Your Fundraising plan brought new donors, kept the ones you have and offered exciting long-term investment in the results of this ministry for major donors

The Dictionary definition of Stability is pretty insightful if you think about it:

sta·bil·i·ty
noun \stə- 'bi-lə-tē
        : the quality or state of something that is not easily changed or likely to change
        : the quality or state of something that is not easily moved
        : the quality or state of someone who is emotionally or mentally healthy

First, "not easily changed" could be a good thing.

Consider what it would mean if your staff felt like it was a safe place to work. Your volunteers felt that their time was well invested. People knew that your message and your actions were aligned.

Second, "not easily moved" might mean "consistent", "lasting", and "dependable." As a ministry, you need to be consistent so that people begin to trust you.

The real question about Stability is whether you believe the strategic plan is what God has on His copy or not. If it is, when things get "tight" you need to get "closer" and allow God to show Himself as He provides. In my experience, He will provide for the needs in ways that you may not have expected. (Luke 14:28-30)

Far too often though, ministries get scared and begin chasing money. They end up getting "off mission." This type of instability can lead to an erosion of trust with your donors, volunteers and staff.

By "Chasing Money" I mean that some ministry leaders get fearful when the bank account gets low and begin chasing money to "fix it." How sad that rather than going to Dad and asking to see Him provide, we forget who their Provider is in the first place. (Proverbs 3:5, 6)

As a result of chasing money, when a new "Major Donor" opportunity is presented, whatever the donor wants to give to can become the new "Plan." At that point, you are trading Stability for certainty and your faith just got a lot smaller.

By sticking with the Strategic Plan, you will be able to focus on what you need the money for, and under what circumstances you would turn the offer of funding down. The main question in these situations is: "Does this gift help us achieve our already stated strategic agenda, or not?"

If not, it's time to practice your graciousness and decline to accept the offer. Every gift should align with the approved budget and the mission of the ministry. (During one of our rescue mission capital campaigns, we actually sent a $50,000 check back to a company famous for brewing beer. Sometimes, it's not really about the money.)

Rather than chasing funding, wouldn't it make more sense to live within what God provides and not get ahead of His provision? What if your annual budget depended upon what came in last year plus what's in the bank that you didn't spend?

Can you keep the doors open and still serve the folks you are called to serve?

None of this means that you shouldn't have a professional and effective fundraising plan. In fact, if you don't have a plan, you will never see God use it to bring His response to your prayers.

Another area where this comes into play is the area of Planning and commitments.

If you have taken the time to seek God's direction and then crafted a strategic plan around that "Vision" you owe it to God and yourselves to follow that plan as closely as you can. Many a ministry has gone off the rails because they had a "great idea" presented to them and it wasn't part of the Master Plan they have been given.

Remember - Sometimes growth should not be the goal!

Just because you can't serve all the people that need your help doesn't mean you should run your organization so lean that you can't do good work for the people you can serve.

Why water down the soup if the nutrition is what is needed for those who you can provide the meal to – today. God is big enough to take care of the ones you can't help – or He will provide more resources so that you can serve them with the same quality you have committed to in your strategic plan.

Ask yourself why you feel the need to grow. Could it be that you should focus more energy on Excellence in all areas of the ministry – and only grow when you have too much need and too many resources for your current location?

Finally, the state of being "Emotionally or Mentally Healthy"

Here is where it might get personal for some of us.

Remember Alex? What type of person is Alex likely to be attracted to? Would he connect well with an "Aggressive Preacher" or "convert-hunting Bible-thumper" or would he be more likely be attracted to a humble, confident friend that gets to know him on a personal level?

I'm not saying you shouldn't evangelize. What I'm saying is that when it comes time to present the Gospel, follow the example of Jesus. Yes, He taught openly to the masses – but they followed Him to hear from him. I haven't found a passage yet that indicates that Jesus ever stood on a street corner and proclaimed doom to anyone but the religious leaders of the day.

Instead, I read that He spent time with sinners, getting to know them and allowing them to know Him. He offered healing and forgiveness to those who were at the end of their rope as a friend would who is helping you out of the pit you just fell into.

The sky is never falling; there is no power struggle in Heaven for the souls of men. God has already won the day through Christ, and we owe it to this culture to present that confidence, that assurance, and that clear story.

The real question is to ask yourself what you are doing to make Salvation sound like a good thing. Do the rewards seem clear and attainable to the Alex's out there?

The final thought on Stability is that there are 7 areas of Operational Quality (Excellence) that need to be established and maintained. We will cover them in detail later, but for now, they are:

1. Legal Activities
2. Governance and Leadership
3. Planning and Evaluation
4. Human Resources – Staff & Volunteers
5. Financial Operations
6. Program Delivery
7. Fundraising & Public Relations

You can't do without any of these components and they all need to be working well.

Without all of these areas working well it's like asking God to let you win at Black Jack when you are betting the mortgage money. That doesn't make sense on this planet, and I wouldn't want to have to explain in person why I expected God to make up for my being stupid with His resources.

John Wayne was famous for saying, "Life is hard. It's harder if you're stupid." Wise man - Pilgrim.

When they are working well, you can then focus on doing more significant things in the Kingdom.

SIGNIFICANCE

As more and more people come along side to support the results of the work that God is doing, the resources will come in to provide the solid base of support you need to enter the SIGNIFICANCE phase.

Here you can do new or bigger things. It's the ability to stop "Fixing Things" and start "Doing New Things."

Imagine a day when this stable ministry has enough financial and operational momentum to bring its leadership together and plan for the next big thing.

Perhaps it is a new facility so that you can help more people receive your services and be able to serve them with the quality and Excellence you established in the Stability phase. Or, maybe you will be able to launch satellite campuses so that you can take what is working here – and plant it over there.

LEGACY

Finally, as God brings results, you will need a method to keep His story "The Story" as you enter the LEGACY phase.

How often do you see God at work in your daily routine?

If you are watching closely, a ministry that is Stable and doing Significant things will see His fingerprints on a regular basis. They may look like normal "happens-all-the-time" events, but I'm suggesting that you look at those events and ask a deeper question.

Would this have happened if God hadn't been involved?

You may not be able to answer that very easily, but when in doubt – blame Him for the good stuff. Far too often we've heard ministry personnel say things like, "Oh, that happens all the time. We're used to it." Wow – did they just miss the point!

I suggest that as the ministry leadership, you make a concerted effort to identify the things that only God could have done. Begin collecting those stories – they will come in handy when things are going badly.

In your personal life, I'm sure you can point to a time or place where God intervened in a circumstance and changed the outcome. You need to be capturing the history of God-At-Work in your ministry as well.

Think about the impact at your next board meeting, or staff retreat, or budget meeting. The knowledge that you are not alone, that God is working in and through the ministry, can bring reassurance and comfort when the times are tough – and they will be if you are serving God well.

12   GOD'S FRANCHISE

According to the website, *Entrepeuner.com* (12/14) the fastest growing franchises in America right now are Subway sandwich shops.

For a small investment of from $100,000 to $265,000, plus a $15,000 franchise fee, plus 8% of your sales revenue for the next 20 years, you too can share in the world of adventure of self-employed fast food ownership.

Becoming a Subway franchisee also provides 2 whole weeks of training at the Subway headquarters, advertising material that you can pay to promote, and all the minimum wage teenage employment hassles you ever wanted.

Do they have standards you need to follow? Absolutely! You won't find a Subway offering mac and cheese pizza – no, no. Headquarters tends to frown on being off the menu.

But you'll be in business, and for the most part – a profitable business that affords you the ability to take care of your family. (Assuming you picked a good location)

Subway is becoming so popular that they're popping up on almost every corner like Starbuck's used to.

In fact, if the service isn't very good at this one, you only have to go a few blocks down the street to a "New Store" to get good service. This works because the new store is more focused on quality than the old store because they are trying to win the hearts of everyone that comes in for a sandwich.

Got it?

Now, fellow follower of Christ, what happens if you think of your ministry as one of God's franchises?

- What did you have to invest?
- What were the requirements?
- Are there standards that you have to keep?
- Are you paying Royalties?
- Who should work here?
- How should this be lead?
- Etc … etc …. etc …….

Hopefully, you're getting the point.

Let's assume that God did call you to serve Him. That He did give you a vision. That He does have a plan for your ministry. Wouldn't He have standards and expectations that He would want you to uphold?

I believe that this is exactly why so many small ministries struggle today. Because the focus is on what they are doing for God, not in what God wants to do through them, and quality of their character while they are doing it.

I mentioned this earlier, but your donors and volunteers are following God through your ministry. The standards of professionalism need to be equal to any for-profit organization – with one exception, and it's a big one.

Your Non-Profit Ministry Represents
the God of the Universe!

You are in fact an Outpost of Heaven in a wilderness of self-absorbed relativism and you may be the only picture that some people get of Christ.

How you run the Ministry, and who people believe you are affiliated with is the ultimate issue at stake. Are they getting the right picture?

Is that idea evident when the Alex's of the world look at you? As they listen to the stories of how people's lives are changed through your ministry, are they drawn to the possibility that you had help doing what you do?

Why would they pay attention to your message over all the other "great causes" out there?

My wife and I raised our two children in Orange County, California. I was privileged to work with the Union Rescue Mission in Los Angeles during part of that time. You know what? Between Ventura and San Diego there are dozens of Rescue and homeless ministries. Why would someone invest their hard earned money, time and talent in URM over the others?

Those are the questions that you must answer in a winsome way. Those are the reasons for seeking Excellence in how you present your "Franchise Results" in your newsletter.

But this idea goes beyond the marketing components of newsletters and appeal letters. It strikes at the very heart of who you are as a ministry leader.

The idea of being a *Humble-Servant-Warrior*, able to present our relationship with the God of the Universe without personal guilt, shame or weakness.

This may be the hardest part of what we have had to deal with over our consulting career.

You see, you can spend all the time in the world fixing the operational issues of the ministry only to get to the point where the leadership needs to address weakness in their personal life. When change gets that close to home – it hurts.

This comes into play when the Executive Director can't keep his eyes where they belong when he's around female staff, or a board member who believes their individual agenda is more "divinely inspired" than the other board members, or the staff person who does only the minimum to get by because "we're a non-profit."

You might get the point that I'm angry about these things – and you'd be right. I could tell you story after story of ministries that came to us for advice and counsel only to have one of us end the relationship when it got down to "Personal Character" issues with leadership.

On the positive side though I have just as many stories of how God provides and protects His ministry when the leadership stops doing the ostrich thing and faces the challenges with courage.

God is faithful, He's patient – but He's not kidding. As ministry leaders we are not above reproach, and like Godly leaders of the past – held to a higher standard.

13   BALANCING FAITH AND PROCESS

You are too liberal.

You are too conservative!

How come nobody is ever "Just Right" as in the Goldilocks fable?

Being pressured to take one side or the other, many people attempt to develop "Consensus" to deal with extreme positions. It can be a real problem.

Unfortunately, being middle-of-the-road can get you no where most of the time.   In politics, those in the center are labeled "Bi-Partisan" which for most of us means they can't make a decision or lead.   It would be better for everyone if today's political leaders either said what needed to be said or shut up and went home.

Godly Leaders need to make a decision and lead those who are following into the vision of the future that God gave you.

But what do you base your decisions on?   As a Godly leader, you must pray for wisdom and discernment.   You should get advice from a multitude of counselors.   And then what? God doesn't use fleeces any more – how is a person supposed to know exactly which is the right direction or action.

Does anyone remember the first commercially available spreadsheet programs?

In 1979 Apple launched VisiCalc. It was the first spreadsheet program that you or I could buy. Lotus followed in 1983 by launching 1-2-3 for the MS DOS environment.

At the time, our small Financial Services firm had purchased a brand new Windows AT computer as an upgrade from the double-floppy version. This revolutionary piece of equipment had an internal hard drive that held "15 megabytes" of data. WOW were we on top of the technology curve back then!

But for this new wonderment to be of any use beyond a glorified word processor – we needed to crunch numbers. Enter Lotus 1-2-3 and my love for spreadsheets began.

With a spreadsheet, we could prove our worth. We could calculate fancy returns and project wonderful scenarios of financial bliss far into the future.

At the same time, we could become totally dependent on "Empirical Data" to validate our preconceived notions of our own worth or wisdom. (Painful times – just painful)

What was happening in the Christian ministry sector at the time was noteworthy as well.

Experienced Ministry leaders were embracing this new technology so that they could quantify their fundraising results. Life was getting better because they could project the ROI of a mailing and compare response rates against A/B splits faster and cheaper than ever before.

Here is the important question: *What was happening to their Faith and their ability to hear God's leading?*

There is no real way to measure that – but I'm pretty sure the pendulum was swinging from the extreme of "Whatever God Provides" (Faith) to "We need a higher ROI." (Spreadsheet)

Over thirty years later, I can safely say that neither "extreme" is where God wants us.

Luke 14:28-30 makes it pretty clear that you should have a plan. But is it enough to simply pray or should you use spreadsheets (data) to validate our decisions, and how much weight should either side of the issue get? How do you balance them to get down to what you should call your Plan?

Here is how I have learned to value both positions and not get stuck in the middle – unable to make a decision.

We must merge the mentality of a left brain spreadsheet analyst with a right brain heart driven minister to come up with the correct answer. Neither can function effectively without the other.

In fact, if you have ever taken George Barna's Christian Leader Profile, you probably already know that if you are predominately faith driven and have little to no comfort with spreadsheets you should align yourself with a spreadsheet junkie to get the best decisions out of your planning.

This evaluation tool is worth the $30 investment and delves into your Calling, Character, Competencies and Aptitude as they relate to your Leadership potential. We recommend that every person in a Leadership role in your organization take it and that you don't hire someone whose results might indicate they are not a perfect match with your mission.

(https://www.barna.org/dloads/christian-leader-profile-download-detail)

The reverse holds true as well. If you are a spreadsheet junkie (me) you need to align yourself with a passionate right brained person (my wife) in order to not put too much faith in the numbers themselves.

Both sides need both sides in order to see the entire picture clearly.

One final thought on this way of thinking. You need to remember that God is not committed to your plan. He is committed to His. Your struggle is to know, as well as can be discerned, what His plan is. That's the hard part.

Think about these two methods.

First, your plans need to be written with a proverbial pencil, meaning that if God wants to change them, you shouldn't stand in His way simply because "It's your God-breathed Strategic Plan!" Lighten up and let God drive.

Second, metaphorically, your ministry is a little red wagon that you are pushing down the street. Guess who should be steering? If it's God's plan – exactly – you'll end up right where you thought you would.

If He is changing it, you'll know it in your heart and you'll see it in your spreadsheet.

14   A "MINISTRY 2.0" PERSPECTIVE

So the question before us is, "Why must we talk in terms of Business and Ministry as a combined idea?"

The point should be pretty clear by now that as one of God's Franchise partners – you are in business with God to deliver the services you have been called to deliver. In that capacity, you must run the ministry as a professional organization for the following reasons:

1. You represent the God of the Universe who doesn't do anything half-way

2. Donors, Volunteers, Staff and Board members want to support an exciting, exceptional ministry.

3. Why not?

Let's go through these ideas in a bit more detail.

When God created the heavens and the earth, He put man and woman in the Garden of Eden. Because there was no Sin, He called everything "Perfect." And then the enemy of our soul stepped in and things got all messed up.

As Adam's sin has filtered down to us, Christ came to redeem the fallen creation and restore our relationship with God to the pre-fall environment. The rest of the world still needs to be impacted by effective Christians following the directions Christ gave us in Matthew 28.

The likelihood that we can pull that off on a global scale is pretty weak – but on a one-off scale, your ministry can point to how God transforms the broken sinful nature into something exciting and worthy of admiration. Add to that the idea that when you align your ministry operations with God's blueprint – He is pleased. When God is pleased, you see Him equipping the ministry in ways that only He can do – and that's the main point.

It's all about allowing others to see God through the work He allows you to do. Your attitude and how you apply these ideas need to be aligned with the Centurion in Matthew 8:5 that came to Christ asking that Jesus heal his servant.

Do you remember what Jesus said about this soldier's faith? Matthew 8:10 says in part, *"Truly I say to you, I have not found such great faith with anyone in Israel."* That's the kind of Jesus follower I want to be.

Second, people want to back a winner. If we define winner in Biblical terms, it's a person or organization that represents the *Excellence* we see in God through Christ. We aren't going to get the perfection meter to 100%, but we need to peg that needle as high as possible.

The ability to do this comes from a humble acknowledgement that as adopted sons and daughters, we need to represent the Father well – because we love Him and want Him to be honored.

At the point where we are planning or operating below what we are capable of – we are missing out on the opportunity to present the best possible picture of Christ to the Alexes of the world. He needs to see something that forces him to consider Christ in a new way.

Finally, why wouldn't we try to be more professional? What would that hurt?

In my own business, expedience would sometimes get in the way of taking the few seconds it takes to ask myself this one important question. *"Is this the best I can do or can I do better?"*

Like you, I had to train myself to slow it way down and ask the important questions up front – before launching an idea or concept. Taking that little bit of time makes all the difference later, and the people you serve or the pressing concern will still be there, but now your solution will be better.

I don't want my own laziness or time limits to prevent me from doing something right the first time. Do it well and you don't have to go back a fix it. Time is too precious.

The answer for the busy Leader is to build quality into the plan up front. Do the hard work first before implementing anything. The only reason that we should have to go back to the drawing board is because God is changing the plan and we need to build *Excellence* into the next version.

So does that mean we will always get it right? Unfortunately, no. But it does mean that as we are open to allowing God to lead, He is more involved in the results and the number of "adjustments" are fewer than if we had just slapped something together and launched it.

IBM, Apple, Amazon, Your Ministry – Of all these, Your Ministry should be thought of more highly to those who have experienced you.

Do they know you as people of Christ? Do they feel your love for them? Do they perceive Excellence as a characteristic of your ministry?

If we don't try to reach for that idea – you will always hit something less.

15   THE EXCELLENCE COMPONENTS

We've talked a lot in this book about *Excellence* and its importance as we represent God to a fallen world. Nowhere else do people have the opportunity to see tangible evidence that God is still alive and active than when they look at one of His franchises run with *Excellence*.

The question then is, what goes into Excellence and how should that affect your day to day operations.

First, the idea that God wants us to run the race to win requires that we have a full tool box and that each part of the ministry has what it needs to be aligned with that Excellence.

Second, the people of God, those who represent "C" Christianity, must be committed to bringing Him glory. However your ministry plays out, whomever you serve and whoever is watching, they need to come away with an awareness that you had help beyond your own capabilities.

Third, the foundational underpinnings of your operation need to be solid. No bricks out of place and firmly held together with the mortar of faith and commitment to God's plan.

This is another area where Small ministries should pay more attention.

Do you remember the scripture that warns us in Romans 13:1 telling us to *"be in subjection to the governing authorities?"* Since God establishes who wins the election, in effect, He is telling us what we need to do when a rule or regulation is published. We don't get to choose which edict to follow. Unfortunately, we really have had people tell us that they didn't need to do something (follow some rule) because they were a non-profit. Ignorance (of the law) or arrogance are not excuses that work.

That is what we are talking about, but even more so because we are asking for and expecting God to bless our work.

You need to have your operation working well in all areas.

To do that, you need to be excellent in the following 7 areas:

1 - Legal Activities – Licenses, Contracts, Policies, Filings and Fees all need to be correct and current.

2 - Governance & Leadership – Is your board and Leadership comprised of Godly men and women who exemplify the *Humble-Servant-Warrior* model?

3 – Planning & Evaluation – Is your Strategic Plan current and reviewed annually? If not why not.

4 – Human Resources – Staff and Volunteers – Did you hire the right person for the right reasons and are they performing at a New-Professional-Organization level. Same for volunteers

5 – Financial Operations - Open, Transparent, Accurate and Accountable – How are you doing?

6 – Program Delivery – Are you reaching the right people with the right resources at a cost that is efficient. Are you

stretching too far with the resources you have or should you do more for fewer?

7 – Fundraising, Marketing and Public Relations – Capturing the stories, telling the stories, creating the opportunities, stewarding the donors, reaching every audience possible. Building relationships and trusting God for the results – how are you doing?

These "tangible" tools blended with your intangible tools of faith, Godliness, prayer, tenacity, professionalism, humility, grace, style, diligence – these are the components of a truly "C" Small Christian Ministry that can run with Excellence and draw many new people to the conversation.

16   How To's

Excellence, Quality, Better– all these words boil down to just one simple idea.

It's the notion that doing "ministry" at the highest level requires a solid commitment from the ministry leadership.

As one of God's Franchisees, your mission is to deliver the highest possible impact for the people you serve while at the same time directing the glory and fame to God who is making the impact possible.

For most of us, that's not an easy task on a day-to-day basis. In fact, I/we get tired and simply want "life" to settle down and not contain so much pressure.

"Dan, isn't what you are saying going to take more work and make life harder?" Well, in the short-term yes, but it's definitely worth it.

Some of us came from the for-profit sector before joining full-time ministry work. Some came right into ministry from college or other pursuits. Whichever path you took, you probably experienced your fair share of trial and error during that time. Some ideas were clearly better than others as time and experience proved.

Ultimately, we learn from those episodes and bring a keener understanding of what it takes to run a ministry when we make the transition.

Now, think back. Did you ever have anything work out beyond expectation purely by accident? Probably not. Those experiences most likely took the most planning and effort.

So it is in the life of running a Franchise. Unlike the Subway franchise, you don't get an operations manual that tells you how to do all of this stuff. Instead, you get a Bible that tells you who to be while you do all this stuff.

God has expectations of Quality and Excellence for us – as His people. He then indicates that we are fools if we don't do the heavy lifting (planning for Excellence) before we start doing things in His name.

So here we are at the Commitment concept and we need to decide what to commit to – exactly. We can make the default decision or we can make the Excellence decision.

My position is that I would rather put the energy in up front, before I invest other resources. In other words, I'm willing to work very hard up front so that the rest of the concept comes off smoothly and efficiently.

How many times have we had to go back and repair something that could have been taken care of earlier? It's waist! Nobody likes losing time or money they didn't need to lose.

Now, if you are the CEO or Board Chair, what do you do to (a) make the decision toward Excellence and (b) get your team on board?

As you might suspect, Excellence cannot be "sold" as a label we put on our work. It needs to be the recognized observations that others make about us. Let me say that another way. People need to perceive the Excellence as they watch what the ministry does and how it does it. It can't be what we say – it has to be what people see us do.

For me, this means that I'll try my hardest to deliver Excellence within the resources I have and keep my eye on how to make things better in every area of my work. Not with a judgmental tone but one of bringing higher expectations and goals to my team as a way of ultimately making our work easier.

That may also mean that I have multiple plans to reach different levels of Quality or Excellence over time – but the overarching goal is improvement.

For instance, what if you don't have the budget for the newfangled thingy that would save you some wonderful amount of money.

If you can't write a check for it right now you probably can't afford it. It may mean that you need to be content delivering A- quality now, while you commit to saving and investing for the ability to purchase that A+ capability in the near future? (Patience is wonderful except for how long it takes to get)

So the first commitment is to Excellence as something that God wants from us.

But the second commitment is to Excellence as something that I want for me. What are our Christian-self-interests when it comes to improving the quality of everything in the ministry?

Well, again, it gets down to two things. God's reputation in a culture that thinks He's dead, and my eternal reward.

Picture this with me. Your ministry's name was just announced at the Reward Ceremony in Heaven. You are on your way to the podium to meet Christ who will be giving you the reward He promised for working with this ministry.

According to Revelation 5, you and I will reign with Christ for eternity. We'll be given responsibilities that are commensurate with our skills and stewardship.

Now, I don't have a clue about what that will look like, but as with all things God designs, it's probably better than we can image on this side of the fence.

Let's assume that the level of quality and Excellence you inject into His franchise now impacts your responsibilities in Heaven? Would that change how you feel about your workload now?

What if, along with the "normal" rewards for praying, giving and going – God adds things to our reward based upon His assessment of our ability to be the *Humble-Servant–Warriors* He called us to be?

I can imagine that the quality of our work is graded and our reward "amplified" as a result. Some things you have to take on faith. That's probably one that will surprise us.

Oh yeah, one final thought on commitment. In the infamous words of a short green guy (Yoda), "No try – Do!"

Commitment isn't a test drive of an idea.

Commitment is being sold out and investing everything to make it happen. It's not always going to be easy and it will challenge our faith – but those aren't bad things if we want God to bring His blessings into His ministry.

I think they are worth the effort in the long-run.

17   IF WE COULD JUST "STOP!"

A Hamster, Gerbil, Lab Rat running a never ending race to nowhere, that's how you feel. There is always something more that needs to be done – by you – right now!

What if you just stopped for a day? Would the world stop spinning? Bet it wouldn't.

There are never enough hours or days or weeks in a month are there? How can we best handle all that comes to our desks in an excellent manner? The pressure to just get through it makes us take the comfortable and familiar route to solving the problem. We never get the time to work on Quality.

I don't want to over-simplify things in this regard. The work you are doing is critical to the fulfillment of the mission. People are counting on you to get it done and done right. But friend, you had better make time to think before you explode.

I have two thoughts on this that come from personal and professional experience.

First, a pastor suggested something one Sunday that has helped clarify many of my personal and professional decisions.

He said, "To really hear God, you have to slow it way down. Be in a place where the busyness ends and the listening begins." I thought that was pretty good advice.

For many leaders, that's why they go on Leadership Retreats or go to Conferences with like-minded folks. My experience is that all we are doing in those instances is trading one type of pressure (to get things done) for another (to figure out how to get things done). That doesn't seem very productive.

I like the mountains. Growing up next to the Sierra Nevada Mountains in California probably ruined me for dessert oasis vacations, but that's where I feel His presence in a tangible way. I can walk down a path or sit on a rock overlooking a valley or stream and imagine God the Father sitting next to me. Dad and I having some quality time together.

It's a place where I can listen. Where I can pour my heart out and no one is there to ask intruding questions. Just Dad and I.

In one of those mountain top visits I came away with a very clear understanding that part of my mission of inspiring Excellence in Christian Ministry leaders was to remind them (you) to intentionally schedule time to work "On" your ministry instead of "In" it.

There is a big difference between the two as you probably know already. And there-in lies the problem. It's not a matter of you not knowing this already. You've read all the books and blogs, been to all the seminars and conferences and still you are building up pressure that is about to blow.

The issue is the need to create a discipline in your life where you schedule (decide) the time to turn off the volume and listen to the message. That's hard to do. So let's take a stab at it together:

It begins by realizing that not all principles from the business world come directly from Satan's desk. In fact, many of you clearly see business concepts and practices in Scripture – and work to apply them in your ministry. Good for you! Keep it up.

Others, however, do not or cannot translate them into Ministry applications. Things are clearly broken. Low staff morale, missed deadlines, and an overall sense of "this is too hard" seem all too easy to find.

Why is this? Again, you are most likely caught in the trap of working "In" your ministry rather than "On" it. What I mean is that working "On" the ministry forces you to look at the daily, monthly and annual plan as a business plan. Something you need in order to get everyone on the same page.

In the for-profit world, we study four areas in order to get better results:

- Knowledge: - The things you need to know to produce a great product
- Attitudes: - Who you are in reality and perception that makes you function as a team and makes you attractive to your customers
- Skill: - The things you need to do to produce that great product
- Habits: - Your ability to integrate vision, mission, and values in your daily work at all levels of the company

Now let's convert this to the Ministry Environment:

- What is your Product?

- Who are your Customers?
- Is your Staff a Team?
- Is your Strategic Plan being held up as the Ministry Vision at all levels?

If the answer to any of these questions is no, you probably need to carve out some time and put on your "Donald Trump – Ministry Leader" cap and ask yourself questions like:

- If most small ministries don't have the funding they need, why do they keep asking themselves (peer networks and boards) for advice?

- What would have to change in you personally (the leader) in order for that change to filter down to your staff?

- When was the last time your Strategic Plan and your Case for Support were compared to make sure they are in alignment?

- How much time are you spending thinking in New Ways about the ministry? Have you put limits on it by default?

I suggest that if you are the head of your ministry, or the head of your department, these questions should bring you to a point of assessing where you are and how Christ is reflected through you and the ministry.

Do your customers (donors) see a commitment to quality? Do your Vendors like doing business with you? Are your staff members growing closer to Christ and each other?

By working "On" the ministry – you may just get to a place where working "In" the ministry is more rewarding and fun. Now how happy would Christ be with that?

SERVING AS "GOD'S FRANCHISE"

One of the great aspects of buying that Subway franchise we talked about earlier is that you get all the operational manuals, marketing guides, budget pro-formas and document templates you will need to run your franchise within the standards that are prepared by headquarters.

For you to be able to operate your ministry using the principles we've just laid out, you're going to need something similar. You'll need a roadmap and a set of documents that can get you on track and keep you there.

Unfortunately, your Franchise doesn't come with those. Instead, it comes with the knowledge that you are partnered with the God of the universe which is better but not easier. You need to discover His blueprint and put it into action. It will be worth the effort in the end.

In this section we'll be diving into "Strategic Elements" that are needed in order to function as God's franchise.

We'll begin by looking at what we call the 7 Pillars of Excellence. These are the components of your Operational Plan that need to be well designed and functioning at full capacity in order for you to establish the Stability of the ministry and keep it that way.

Stability is the idea that when parts are missing from your car's motor, it runs rough. It sputters and doesn't have the horsepower the engineers designed it to have.

Imagine you just bought a Ford Shelby GT500 Mustang with the 662 horsepower eight cylinder beast under the hood. Now go out to your garage and take out half of the spark plugs. It might start and get you to work tomorrow, but I guarantee it will be running rough and everyone that sees you struggling down the road will wonder what's wrong with you – not your car – with you. That's not a pretty thought if you are a car guy like I am.

Now transfer that thought to your ministry. What happens when the Staff or the Board or the Volunteers can't really tell the story of what God is doing, or worse, they tell different stories? What happens when the donors can't perceive your professionalism because the time it took to do excellent planning and presentation wasn't made a priority by the leadership? That's why you need to get the Stability concept up to full strength.

Next, you'll have to get your great "God is involved" stories in front of as many new people as possible while nurturing your existing followers. Marketing the ministry isn't God's job – it's yours. Effective marketing requires a well-crafted plan that creates opportunities for people who don't know anything about you to Know, Like and Trust you.

After a good plan and great marketing, we'll turn to the Funding of your ministry. This is where the balance of faith and process will come together. It is critical that you plan with Proverbs 16:9 in mind. *"The mind of a man plans his way, but the Lord directs his steps."*

To be understood correctly, this concept needs to mean that God is the ultimate provider – but our part is to offer as many people as possible the opportunity to participate in what is going on. That means that we'll need every component of a professional fundraising plan to be working at its best.

Finally, our franchise plan requires Leadership that gets it. The "It" in that statement is the idea that there are separate and distinct roles for the Board to play as the ministry serves with Excellence.

If you have the right people on the Board, they need to understand and apply their unique skills and wisdom as Trustees and Stewards of the ministry – beyond management of the CEO. That would mean that the board needs to be skilled and polished at blending their ministry hearts with their business heads so that the Trustee-Steward role engenders Godly counsel and management of the CEO – who they are the chief cheerleader for.

Bringing these components together gets you where you need to be. But then what?

To answer that correctly, let me say that what you should be after is this:

- When your existing donors look at your ministry –they should feel good because they are backing a winner

- When potential donors look at your ministry –they should sense that you, above all others in your field, are impacting more people for the money than your competitors

- When you come to work, your Staff should have a sense that God showed up today as well

18   THE 7 PILLARS OF EXCELLENCE

Imagine building a house.

If you've ever built one, you know how much effort and expense goes into it. Some of the first evidence that construction has begun is when the land is cleared, pipes are laid for sewer, water and electrical services and trenches are dug for the foundation.

Next come forms and pads for the foundation and support piers.

The foundation of a house is where it gets its strength. Everything that rests on top of a foundation that should be solid - immovable. All the weight of the building depends on it to resist catastrophe from floods, earthquakes, fire and erosion.

But what if the foundation isn't solid? Things that rest upon it won't be stable will they. In fact, cracks in the foundation let water and pests enter the building eroding its long-term viability. Ultimately, without some major renovations, the building will be uninhabitable.

Ministries are like houses in some interesting ways.

First, your ministry is "home" to the Franchise that God launched. It is the home base of the staff and volunteers who call it their place of ministry. It is home to the future of where God is taking your ministry. It is the home of emotional investment by your donors who invest in its future.

It is an important place. Hopefully, your ministry has taken the time to assure itself that the foundation of the ministry was built correctly in the beginning and is still solid.

Unfortunately, many small ministries seem to always be struggling over one thing or another. Not enough time, money, people, equipment. Too much pressure, uncertainty. Too many interruptions, things to do that never get done, etc . . . .

It doesn't have to be this way.

Again, Luke 14:28-30 reminds us that only a fool tries to build something without proper planning, and if he can't finish it, Christ's reputation, as well as the leaders are tarnished.

In order to prevent this, or repair it, we need to draw your attention to what we are calling the 7 Pillars of Ministry Excellence.

The first pillar looks at **Legal Activities**. After getting your ministry incorporated and a tax exemption obtained, this area deals with whether you are following all the laws and regulations that relate to your community, state and country.

The second pillar identifies your **Governance and Leadership**. How you govern the ministry and lead the people involved needs to be clear and transparent to everyone involved. Whether you choose to be a Policy Board or something else, the primary issues evolve around:

- Are the right people leading the ministry? Faith filled men and women of God who share a love for all that this ministry is and could be?

- Do the Board and Executive Director understand who their provider is? What is their Theology? Is it consistent with Biblical Stewardship – not just in fundraising but in how the trash is taken out and how the hiring process protects and encourages the hiring of the right people? (Appendix – A)

- Is there a God inspired Vision that must be met? Can you tell that story in a compelling and exciting way? Can you answer the "Who Cares" question?

The third Pillar addresses **Planning and Evaluation**. Strategic planning and Evaluation are critical components of knowing whether God is directing or limiting your activities. If something isn't coming about that you firmly believe God wants you to do, you need to allow for the idea that it must be written down in a planning document. You then need to establish a set of evaluation methods to see whether the plan, as it was conceived, is still what God wants to do. Limitations and Blessings are how God moves us around the map. The map is the Strategic Plan.

The fourth pillar focuses on **Human Resources – Staff and Volunteers**. One of the more critical elements of running a ministry that is known for Excellence is the ability to identify, hire and retain qualified staff. Nobody wants to hire, manage, then fire someone that just wasn't the right fit – or worse yet – hired because they would accept your under-market pay rate. It would be better to hire more productive professionally minded people who can get more done for a better rate of pay.

The area of Volunteers is maybe even more important in that they come to you without expectation of compensation. They want to be there. Is there enough to keep the right ones coming back and brining their friends? Time is a major investment in your ministry. You need to treat them as Major Donors. Do you have a plan for that?

The fifth pillar is that of the **Financial Operations**. How is the money handled? Is everything open and above reproach? Does your board member sell insurance to the ministry for a commission and do you have a Conflict-of-Interest Disclosure signed? How money is handled is probably closer to Gods heart than most other things in the Ministry.

The sixth pillar deals with **Program Delivery**. World class services from a non-profit should not be an oxymoron. The only difference between you and a for-profit corporation is that they pay taxes and you are supposed to do more with the money you don't pay in taxes. Excellence and Quality should be what you are known for.

The seventh pillar supports **Fundraising, Marketing and Public Relations**. This pillar tends to get more attention than the others, but here you need a strategy for how to tell the stories of God at work through your ministry. You then need all the elements of professional Fundraising, Marketing and Public Relations to present those stories.

Here is why this look at the 7 Pillars is so important.

If we really are trying to have God pleased with us, and if He has called us to run His ministry as though it were one of His Franchises, we need to be sure that all of the components that are expected in any great company are present and operating at full capacity.

If there is one thing I have learned after many years in business, it is that God isn't there to make up for my failures – that I caused because I was too stubborn to deal with them. I have to do my part before He will do His.

Remember, Proverbs 3:5,6 says:

> *"Trust in the Lord with all your heart and do not lean on your own understanding. In all your ways acknowledge Him and He will make your paths straight."*

The fairly obvious conclusion is that I have to do my three parts and then I can rely on Him to do His. I haven't found that He does the straight path part if I'm not paying attention to my issues.

That's why you need all the parts of your ministry working with Excellence so that having done all you know to do, and having done it well, you have nothing that stands in the way of God doing His part.

This isn't a method of "controlling God" by doing your part as much as it is a way of keeping Him from having to correct you.

I'm guessing that when He's not correcting – He's blessing.

19   MARKETING THE FRANCHISE

When you purchase a Subway sandwich shop franchise, you immediately benefit from all of the Goodwill and Brand Identity they have built over the years. Everyone knows Subway and everyone instantly knows what Subway is all about. It makes selling sandwiches a simple matter of keeping your location clean, staffed with people that seem to care and making sure you picked the right location in the first place.

It's like that in most ministries as well. For the casual observer all Rescue Missions look alike and do the same things and they are usually downtown in the worst part of town. All Pregnancy Centers or Christian Schools or Overseas Missions or (you get the point). The unique differences between ministries can evaporate pretty quickly when one does something that doesn't lift all of them up. (You know what I mean)

How much goodwill and brand identity your particular ministry has is not always clear. Finding out requires market research, time and money. Add to that Social Media, the pressure to increase your ROI from direct mail, the constant call to "Serve more people" and the frustration level just seems to keep rising.

Marketing that is done in a Professional manner involves the process of getting the people who aren't aware or involved with you to Know, Like and Trust you. The entire intent is to generate opportunities for some level of involvement with your mission. (Not necessarily to give you money before they have experienced you, buy the way)

More small ministries fail in this one area than in most other areas. But there is another problem. Your Franchise is one of God's outposts for impacting unreached people for Christ. It seems that marketing on a professional level should be one of your highest priorities.

Now, notice I didn't say sales. I said marketing. The difference is simple. A sale does not take place until proper marketing has positioned your value to a person who has an interest in that value. When that person wants what you offer, when they understand what they get in exchange for their money – that's when they either *Try* something you offer or *Buy* something you offer.

I am using secular marketing terms intentionally to bring this importance into focus. Our marketing must be done at a level that competes effectively against all the other messages – and against all the other ministries – yet with humble confidence and winsomeness that attracts people to your mission.

What do you have to offer that a person can "Try?" Something they can experience without needing to make a large commitment of time or money. I'm guessing that your next mountain top session with God should include that question.

Then, after they have tried your (whatever), what is your strategy that gets them to evaluate "Buying" your (whatever)? Obviously we're using the word Buy as an alternative to Give, either their time or their money.

This critical segment of your Strategic Plan needs to be coordinated with your Public Relations Strategy, your

Advertising plan (direct mail, space ads, etc. . .) and all public messages that anyone from your ministry is allowed to give.

Your Case For Support is the foundational Strategic document that puts all the pre-approved statements, facts, figures, goals and results into one document that is used in all of your "talking points" whether it's your logo or your TV commercials.

This plan should have all the professional quality of a Harvard MBA strategy and none of the professional manipulation. The last thing God needs is our culture's methods for stretching truth into something He wouldn't recognize.

On the other hand, your ability to capture the fingerprints of His presence and tell credible stories of how He is using you to change and impact lives is what you need to be after. Then those stories need to be told in a way that includes all the professional techniques but with the awareness that your message is about allowing people to see God working through your ministry – not you particularly.

The main ingredients of your Marketing Plan include at a minimum:
- Strategic Plan
- Case For Support
- Communications Plan
- Budget
- PR Strategy
- Fundraising Strategy

The channels you need to use include:

- Direct Mail
- Website
- Social Media
- Paid Advertising
- Networking with Volunteers, Peers and Prospects

For each channel there needs to be a strategic plan that aligns with the Ministry Strategic Plan and the Case for Support. Prioritize your marketing opportunities based upon your budget and take advantage of the free stuff as much as possible.

In addition, you should give as much free information away as possible that can help someone participate in your work without having to give money or go through training. In the homeless arena, you might print certificates for a free meal that can be given to our friends at the freeway on-ramps.

Be creative without getting yourself stuck in analysis-by-paralysis. Make it fun and get your entire team involved. If you can serve the people you are hoping to market to, perhaps they will be receptive when you ask them to get involved at a deeper level.

Finally and most importantly, is the idea that whatever we are doing, we need God's direction and blessing. The resources are few and you want to use them wisely. Pray that God will lead people to you that are most like you and that He will make it clear what techniques you should use based upon your current budget.

Honor Him first and don't "sell." That's were sales come from.

20   FUNDING THE WORK

In 1961, Joseph Heller published Catch-22. A satirical novel about a fictional group of servicemen in World War II who attempt to keep their sanity in the midst of the chaos of war and fulfill their service requirements so that they could return home.

The phrase "Catch-22" has been adopted into the English language referring to a type of unsolvable logic puzzle.

That's where we find ourselves as we dive into how to fund this new professional organization that is now operating with Excellence.

Imagine if George Mueller and DL Moody got together and crafted a Fundraising plan.

Mueller, known for praying and not asking and Moody, known for mailing lots of appeal letters would be right at home as we struggle to blend the faith of fundraising with the process of fundraising. But that's exactly what we need to do.

Let's get the disclaimers out of the way first. I think direct mail and all other components of a professional marketing plan are required for any ministry that wants to reach as many people as possible with their message. I also believe that without Faith, it is impossible to please God.

The concept is pretty simple though. Its' both-and. You do both and let God decide what the outcome is.

First, it costs you nothing to pray except time. So much for that being a problem.

Second, when was the last time one tool in your tool belt dealt with every problem? Never. So you need all the tools of professional Fundraising, PR and Marketing working in a coordinated effort, watered by prayer to see what God wants to do.

The Catch-22 part is how all that comes together. Here is how I've done it with major donors over the years. It works in all other areas of funding as well.

The ministry wants the new Development Director to raise $1,000,000 this year. The DOD knows that she's only as good as God is active, so she feels stuck. What if God has a different (meaning lower) number in mind. She'll be accused of not trying hard enough and lose her job, the ministry will be hurt and the enemy will win. If God provides over that number, the Board will expect it again next year. She can't promise those kind of results.

The concern here is that the ministry leadership is dictating a number and they had better support her with all the tools in the tool belt so that she has the highest possibility of raising that money.

Unfortunately, most don't - leading to the average tenure for new development officers of eighteen months. Without resources, strategy or help the poor DOD can't raise enough funding to cover her own salary and the Board decides that it was the person who failed. It's a no win.

But I think there is another issue here at play. It's the idea that the needs of the ministry, as presented by the VP for Finance or the Board, indicate that if we don't raise that amount of money, we'll have to serve fewer people – and we can't let that happen!! Or worse yet, God is somehow required to meet our Fundraising Plan because "our board prayed about the number."

Here is the stark reality. God will give you the money He wants you to have. That's it.

Yes, you should be a diligent steward of the ministry and put appropriate resources into professional Marketing and Fundraising, but at the end of the day, what you get is what God wants you to have and nothing you can do will change that.

The real problem is the dependence ministries have on the process or the faith and not the blend. You can't get chocolate milk without mixing the chocolate syrup with the milk. It needs to be blended.

In the major donor conversation – it's a three-way conversation. As the DOD, she is responsible to tell the stories of how God is using this Ministry to impact lives. She can only control the number of those conversations and that part of her work needs to be tracked and measured.

The donor's part is to respond to the opportunity by giving or not giving based upon what God leads them to as a conclusion. And it's Gods job to motivate and influence both people that He is the one that is leading this dance.

At the end of the day, small Christian ministries need to be content with what God provides, able to capture great stories of how He is using them to impact people and find opportunities to tell those stories to more people than they did last year.

What ends up in the checkbook is God's responsibility. Thank Him and go back to work!

But work on what? Here are the three components of the Donor Mentality as it relates to why people give. All three have to be in place or the gift won't come.

Let's break them down:

1. **An Important Cause**
   The best way to understand this is that the cause has to be important to the potential donor. You need to find out, without sales pressure or manipulation, what God is calling the donor to do with their resources and then have the faith that if God wants them to give to you, they will.

2. **Credible Leadership**
   Donors need to feel and perceive that those in charge are Godly leaders who listen to God's direction and have the professional skills to steward this ministry with Excellence.

3. **Concern for Your Future**
   If the other two are in place, they need to want your version of the ministry to be able to continue doing what you do. They need a sense that their investment keeps the work going that they invest in.

Obviously, if one piece of this is missing, you will never get their "best gifts."

21   A BOARD THAT "GETS IT"

Over the last 25 years, I have had the opportunity to work with many ministries ranging from Rescue Missions, Private Christian Schools, Christian Universities, International Missions Organizations, Urban Mission Programs, Pregnancy and Adoption Agencies and others.

As we've evaluated and guided these ministries, one theme always makes its way to the front of the pack.

Most Ministries Aren't Underfunded – They're Under Lead

What I mean by this is that for the ministries that understand the correct application of Godly Principles, filtered through Godly Men and Women who humbly seek to fulfill Matthew 28:19 – money is usually not a problem. They have just enough to do what really needs to be done with Excellence.

Yes, they could water down the soup and serve more people, but because of their commitment to bringing God's best to the people they serve, they don't. They set a standard for how they will serve these people and allow God to increase or decrease the number based upon what He provides.

These ministries have a Board of Directors that collaborates with the appointed CEO to accomplish a shared vision and plan.

The board's primary functions can be divided into three separate categories:

1. **Trustee/Steward:**   Setting and Approving Governance Policy and Managing the CEO within those policies.

    a. This Board sees their primary role as "Overseers" and "Key Supporters" of the vision and leadership of the CEO.

    b. Their responsibility as Trustee is limited to that of keeping the organization as a whole, and CEO in particular within the approved and published policies that the entire board and CEO have agreed to in advance.

2. **One-Voice:**   This Board speaks as "One" with properly approved Board Minutes to support each directive.

    a. In this environment, no one board member's agenda takes precedence over the group agenda, and no individual board member speaks for the board without approved minutes from a meeting where a quorum is present.

    b. When an individual Board Member speaks for the Board, it is as a Committee Member that has been appointed by the Board at Large to accomplish a specific task within a stated timeframe – and the Board Member's authority is limited to that specific task only.

3. **Resources:**   This Board helps the CEO find, cultivate and obtain the financial resources needed to accomplish the Strategic Plan and Budget. This "Fundraising" is done with a proper understanding of

Biblical Principles of Stewardship and Fundraising
(see Appendix #1)

There are many benefits for the organization and the CEO under these conditions:

1. There is a Board approved budget with which the CEO runs the ministry. Spending and Management authority is vested in the CEO via the approved Budget.

2. Limitations are placed, by board policy, on the expected outcomes and methods for accomplishing the Mission.

3. The CEO is free to operate the ministry within the boundaries set by the policies, and the Trustees function as "Overseers" assuring that the actions of the CEO are within approved policy.

4. New Ministry Initiatives and Strategic Plans are coordinated to assure that money is invested appropriately and that the direction of the ministry stays on track with the agreed upon Mission and Vision.

5. The Staff, Volunteers, and Donors know that the Ministry is being run in a Professional manner with adequate oversight and Stewardship of their financial gifts.

6. Adequate fundraising systems are in place for:

    a. New Donor Acquisition

    b. Annual Donor Development

    c. Major Donor Cultivation

    d. Legacy Giving and Endowment Cultivation

    e. Future Capital Expansion Plans

7. Client Programs have adequate resources including staff and equipment in order to continue serving the Mission of the Ministry.

8. Marketing and Public Relations efforts are coordinated and well planned, giving a consistent message that highlights the "effectiveness of the ministry."

9. Adequate investment is made in the areas of:

    a. Staff Development – Keeping the CEO and Staff current and trained in their professional capacities.

    b. Board Governance – Board Professionalism that includes Recruiting, Training, and supporting overall Board Education.

With these concepts as a backdrop, the effective ministry then has the tools and leadership to cultivate the money needed to operate the Budget.

"A LARGER PODIUM PLEASE"

Definition of podium in English:

noun (plural podiums or podia-dēə)

A small Podium on which a person may stand to be seen by an audience, as when making a speech or conducting an orchestra.

verb

[no object] chiefly US

(Of a competitor) finish first, second, or third, so as to appear on a podium for an award: I've had great results in the sprint and I've podiumed in the individual

Source:
http://www.oxforddictionaries.com/us/definition/american_english/podium
4/1/15

One of the thoughts I have about the Reward Ceremony in Heaven is how long it's going to take. I'm pretty sure we are underestimating how many people will be called to the Podium when your ministry's name is called.

I had an experience early on in my fundraising career that changed my perspective about ministry. It was while I serving as a Major Donor and Planned Giving officer with Wycliffe Associates, one of the Wycliffe Bible Translators ministries.

It was my responsibility to visit with existing major donors and invite them to support the new Ministry Center in Orlando.

As such, I found myself in Dallas one bright sunny day. I wasn't prepared for what happened.

As I drove into the park-like community of old brick mansions and tree lined streets, I was struck with the obvious wealth I was surrounded by.

After parking in front of the house where I had an appointment, I prayed, as usual, and walked up the long front walk next to the perfectly manicured lawn.

The front door was massive and through the leaded glass, I could see someone coming to the door even before I rang the doorbell. As the door opened, I was met by a petite well-dressed elderly lady who warmly greeted me and asked me to come in. "Let's sit in the parlor," she said.

There she already had sweet tea in a pitcher with ice cubes in glasses sitting next to fresh cookies that she must have just baked. The house was a museum with tapestries, art and sculptures surrounding us and crystal chandeliers hanging from the ceiling. Obviously, this family had resources.

I began. "May I ask how you got involved with Wycliffe?" I wasn't ready for the answer. With tears welling up in her eyes, she said, "I wanted to be a missionary, but God wouldn't let me. All I can do is give money."

Let that sink in for a minute. "All I can do is give money." As a professional fundraising officer – those words should have been the touchdown; the bull's eye; the nothing-but-net-shot.

But it was the first part of her statement that caught my attention. "I wanted to be a missionary, but God wouldn't let me."

All of a sudden, I was off balance. Everything in my sales training from the financial planning days said to focus on the money part, but she had said something that was deeper and more impactful. "God wouldn't let me."

Trying to regain my composure I asked what she meant.

Fighting back her tears, she began telling me about the application she had submitted to an overseas mission's organization some 40 years earlier. She had all the qualifications and financial support, but because she had been divorced, she wasn't accepted by that agency. She had lost her dream.

Later marring a wonderful Christian man who had owned his own business, together they had found a heart for a short list of Ministries of which Wycliffe Associates was one.

Her husband had passed away almost 10 years prior to our visit, and her legacy was to continue funding God's work as long as she could. Our discussion lasted over two hours.

Here is what I learned in Dallas that day.

1. Just because someone doesn't directly serve inside of the ministry like you do doesn't mean they are less

important to God. Everyone who Serves, Prays and Gives will come to the Podium when your ministry's name is called and all will be rewarded. How large that list will be can be influenced by you.

2. Ministries have a tremendous responsibility to protect against donors feeling like second-class citizens. Everyone is just as important as the other.

3. The donor visit generally isn't about the money. It's about what God is asking them to do about what He is doing in your ministry.

4. I can be pretty small minded some times. I need to allow for the possibility that when I meet with donors, it just might be for their benefit rather than mine.

To this day, I can't remember what happened at the end of our visit, except that I spent more time thanking her for her involvement than we ever did talking about the project. My mission that day was changed into helping her feel "normal" and healthy about her part in what Wycliffe is able to do.

I wonder, if you run your ministry with Excellence, if you do the hard work of aiming higher, will God let you see things from a new perspective? Do you think, even if you miss, He'll be glad you tried?

I bet that He will. I think He's leaning forward cheering you on right now.

What say we get after it - Okay?

APPENDIX - A

Biblical Principles for Stewardship and Fundraising

Christian leaders, including development staff, who believe in the Gospel of Jesus Christ and choose prayerfully to pursue eternal kingdom values (Mt. 6:19-21), will seek to identify the sacred kingdom resources of God's economy within these parameters:[1]

1. God, the creator (Gen. 1) and sustainer of all things (Col. 1:17) and the One "who works within us to accomplish far more than we can ask or imagine" (Eph. 3:20), is a God of infinite abundance (Ps. 50:10-11) and grace (2 Cor. 9:8).[2]

2. Acknowledging the primacy of the Gospel (Rom. 1:16) as our chief treasure (Mt. 13:44), Christians are called to lives of stewardship, as managers of all that God has entrusted to them (1 Cor. 4:1-2).[3]

3. A Christian's attitude toward possessions on earth is important to God (Mt. 6:24), and there is a vital link between how believers utilize earthly possessions (as investments in God's kingdom) and the eternal rewards that believers receive (Phil. 4:17).[4]

4. God entrusts possessions to Christians and holds them accountable for their use, as a tool to grow God's eternal kingdom, as a test of the believer's faithfulness to God, and

as a trademark that their lives reflect Christ's values (Lk. 16:1-9).[5]

5. From God's abounding grace, Christians' giving reflects their gratitude for what God has provided and involves growing in an intimate faith relationship with Christ as Lord of their lives (Lk. 7:36-50).[6]

6. Because giving is a worshipful, obedient act of returning to God from what has been provided (1 Chron. 29:10-14), Christian fundraisers should hold a conviction that, in partnership with the church, they have an important role in the spiritual maturation of believers (James 3:1).[7]

7. The primary role of Christian fundraisers is to advance and facilitate a believer's faith in and worship of God through a Christ-centered understanding of stewardship that is solidly grounded on Scripture (2 Tim. 3:16).[8]

8. Recognizing it is the work of the Holy Spirit that prompts Christians to give (Jn. 15:4-5) (often through fundraising techniques) (2 Cor. 9:5-7, Neh. 1:4-11), fundraisers and/or organizations must never manipulate or violate their sacred trust with ministry partners.[9]

9. An eternal, God-centered worldview promotes cooperation, rather than competition, among organizations, and places the giver's relationship to God above the ministry's agenda (2 Cor. 4:16-18).[10]

10. In our materialistic, self-centered culture, Christian leaders should acknowledge that there is a great deal of unclear thinking about possessions, even among believers, and that an eternal kingdom perspective will often seem like foolish nonsense (1 Cor. 2:14) to those who rely on earthly kingdom worldview techniques (1 Cor. 2:1-5).[11]

When these principles are implemented, that rely on God changing hearts more than on human methods, the resulting joy-filled generosity of believers will fully fund God's work here on earth (Ex. 36:6-7).[12]

Selected References for Biblical Principles for Stewardship and Fundraising

1) Mt. 6:19-21, 33

2) Gen. 1, Ps. 24:1, Col. 1:17, Eph. 3:20, Ps. 50:10-11, Phil. 4:19, 2 Cor. 9:8, Jn. 1:14

3) Rom. 1:16, 1 Cor. 9:23, Phil. 3:8-11, Mt. 13:44, 25:15-30, 1 Cor. 4:1-2, 1 Pet. 4:10

4) Mt. 6:24, 22:37, 1 Tim. 6:10, Phil. 4:17, Prov. 24:12, Mt. 19:27-30, Lk. 14:12-14, 1 Cor. 3, 2 Cor. 5:10, Eph. 2:10, 1 Tim. 6:19

5) Lk. 16:1-9, Rom. 1:1, 2 Cor. 8-9, Gal. 6:10, Col. 3:17, 1 Tim. 6:18

6) Lk. 7:36-50, Gen. 14:20, Ezra 2:69, Mk. 12:41-44

7) 1 Chron. 29:10-14, Rom. 12:1, James 3:1

8) 2 Tim. 3:16, Ex. 34:32, 35:21

9) Jn. 15:4-5, Is. 55:8-11, 2 Cor. 9:7, 1 Chron. 28:6, 29:9, Ps. 90:17, Prov. 21:1, 2 Cor. 3:5

10) 2 Cor. 4:16-18, Ps. 90:1-12

11) Cor. 2:14, 1 Cor. 2:1-5, 1 Cor. 1:17-31

12) Ex. 36:6-7, Mt. 6:10

ABOUT THE AUTHOR

Dan (Daniel J) Mirgon is the founder and President of Dan Mirgon & Associates, Inc., an international consulting firm specializing in helping small Christian ministries establish Operational Stability, turn that into Significant Impact for the people they serve, and create a Legacy of God's involvement in the ministries he works with.

His firm was founded in 1991 after he left the financial services industry where he was a Registered Investment Advisor and Financial Planner serving successful business owners and professionals in Orange County, California.

Joining the Union Rescue Mission in Los Angeles as the Director of Estate and Charitable Gift Planning, Dan was instrumental in establishing the URM Foundation, a support organization of the largest Rescue Mission on the west coast. He also served in Major Donor and Planned Giving leadership roles with Wycliffe Associates and Biola University.

Later attaining the Certified Fundraising Executive certification, Dan's firm serves large and small ministries throughout the United States and Canada.

The mission of Dan Mirgon & Associates, Inc. is

To Inspire and Support Small Ministry Excellence so that people see God at work and either join what He is doing or reconsider their view of Him because of what they see.

Dan and his wife Sue live in Salt Lake City, UT and have two grown children and two grandchildren.

To learn more about Dan Mirgon & Associates, Inc. please visit DMA's website at:

www.mirgonconsulting.com or call 888.633.5422

LIST OF REFERENCES

Barna, George, *The Seven Faith Tribes: Who They Are, What They Believe, and Why They Matter*, Carol Stream, IL, Tyndale House Publishers, Inc., 2009

Barna, George, Christian Leader Profile: https://www.barna.org/dloads/christian-leader-profile-download-detail

Thrall, Bill; McNicol, Bruce; Lynch, John, *TrueFaced: trust God and others with who you really are.*, Colorado Springs, CO, NavPress, 2004

Young, Wm. Paul, *The Shack: Where Tragedy Confronts Eternity*, Los Angeles, CA, Windblown Media, 2007

www.ingramcontent.com/pod-product-compliance
Lightning Source LLC
Chambersburg PA
CBHW062023200326
41519CB00017B/4899